The MacDowalls

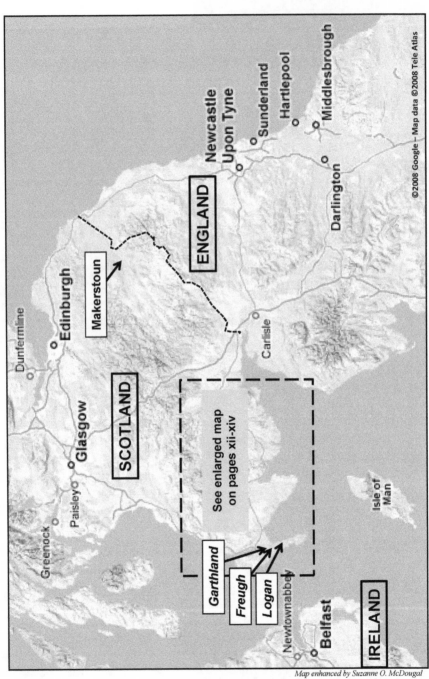

The MacDowalls

Fergus D. H. Macdowall
and
William L. MacDougall

Clan MacDougall Society of North America, Inc.

Clan MacDougall Society of North America, Inc., Parkton 21120
    www.macdougall.org

Copyright 2009 by Clan MacDougall Society of North America, Inc.

ISBN 978-0-578-02679-4

Library of Congress Control Number: 2009905060

Cover:
    Background: MacDowall Tartan
    Design: Suzanne O. McDougal
    MacDowall Badge: From Clan MacDougall website
    Text: William L. MacDougall

This book is printed on acid-free paper.

Contents

Editors and Contributing Writers v

Foreword.. vii

Introduction ix

Ancient History of the MacDowalls.. 1

Troubled Years 9

Struggles... 14

Makdougals of Makerstoun.. 20

Macdowell/M'dowall of Stodrig 37

MacDougall/Macdowall of Lodvica, Duwall, and von Wahl................. 43

Westward Exodus... 52

Settlement in Early Colonial America... 55

McDowells of Virginia and Kentucky.. 63

To Virginia and the Carolinas: The Great Wagon Road 73

Toward Revolution... 83

MacDowalls in the U.S. Civil War... 96

Thain MacDowell: Hero.. 102

MacDowell Descendants in Russia 110

Journeying in MacDowall Country 115

MacDowalls of Note.. 125

Castles, Towers, and Other Fortifications 130

Abbeys of the Lords of Galloway... 150

Names and Spellings Connected to MacDowall 160

Bibliography 161

Contact Us 168

Maps
    Overview.. ii
    Galloway .... xii-xiv

Editors and Contributing Writers

Fergus D. H. Macdowall ---------------------------- Editor-in-Chief

William L. MacDougall ---------------------------- Editor

Scott A. MacDougald ---------------------------- Associate Editor

Suzanne O. McDougal ---------------------------- Production Editor

❋ ❋ ❋

René A. van Iterson

W. Lesley McDowall

Kenth Berg

Henning von Wahl

Leo B. McDowell

Linda McDowell Swann

Vitaliy Negoda

Walter M. Macdougall

Foreword

In 2004, Fergus Macdowall and I met in Oban, Scotland, during an international gathering of the Clan MacDougall. I asked him about my growing suspicion (later confirmed) that my ancestors, who emigrated from Kelso, Scotland, to America in 1796, were actually MacDowalls. Fergus considered the evidence and said that, yes, my family was probably from the Makdougals of Makerstoun (near Kelso)—an old branch of the MacDowalls.

Fergus had contributed to my book, *Kings in the West Beyond the Sea: An Informal History of the Clan MacDougall*, and we began to talk about the possibility of working on a similar volume about the MacDowalls. Years later, this book, with the help of an array of gifted authors from around the world, is the result. Fergus and I hope it is the beginning of a continuing effort—possibly with future editions—to record the movements and accomplishments of an ancient and distinguished family that has left an indelible mark on civilization the world over.

William L. MacDougall
Editor
2009

Introduction

The ancestry of the MacDowalls, as for all Gaels, goes back in antiquity to the origins of the Celts. That race evolved during several millennia B.C. from Stone Age, pre-proto-Celtic, nomadic Indo-Europeans on the steppes of Russia.

Their metallic materials were drawn chiefly from Ireland, so about 300–50 B.C. a preeminent family/clan of the Goedelic-speaking Celts of Iberia in the Spanish peninsula migrated as Milesians to invade and settle in southern Ireland. They quickly overcame the indigenous races, and ultimately developed their own branches of five kingdoms vying in Tara for the high-kingship of the nation.

After eight centuries of internecine feuds, a senior branch from the original landing site in Kerry was led by Carbri Riada to the northeast of Antrim and established the 30-mile-long coastal kingdom of Dal Riada.

After a century of probing the Pictish shores of Alba, the Dalriadan grandsons of King Erc, namely Lorne, Fergus, and Angus, attacked the Picts with force to establish the Scottish Dalriadan kingdom in 503 A.D. Long lines of kingship continued down to King Alpin who in 741 was killed in Galloway while possibly seeking Irish and Norse support against Oengus, king of the Picts, who were driving the Dalriadans back to the Western Isles and Ireland only to be overwhelmed by the invading Norse. The latter, as Norwegians and Danes, took the suzerainty of the Isles and Ireland, but maintained the Scots Dalriadans as governors of the Gaels.

Alpin, of the dominant Fergus-Gabran line of kings in Argyll, succeeded Dungal, also named Dougal—the only Dalriadic king named Dougal—from our more senior House of Loarn in Lorn. After Alpin's defeat by a Galwegian-Angle force he was ultimately succeeded by Kenneth MacAlpin who grew up in Galloway and united the Scots and Picts in the kingdom of Scotia (844). For his purpose, he used primarily Galwegians to whom he gave the privilege of forever leading the van (front) of Scottish armies, but he did not wrest Scots Dalriada from the Norse.

Gille was the native Gaelic governor of the Western Isles and Norse-Ireland in 1014 when his brother-in-law, Jarl Sigurd "The Stout," Earl of Orkney, lost Ireland in the Battle of Clontarf at Dublin. The native histories indicate that Gille was the great-grandfather of Fergus Macgille, the first feudal Lord of Galloway, and great-grandfather-in-law of Somerled Macgillebride, Lord of Argyle under King David I of Scotland. That battle and these men led a resurgence of the Scots Gaels in Scotland. However, the Normans of Viking stock under William, Duke of Normandy, conquered the Saxons of England in 1066 and brought in their feudal laws with reinforced Roman Catholicism. Both agendas were enthusiastically enforced by the Prince of Cumbria, David, King of Scotland, who was trained in the court of William's son, King Henry I of England.

Fergus, descended from the Gaels (which David was not), was similarly trained in Henry's court and was granted Henry's natural daughter in marriage—the same treatment given to King Alexander I, David's older brother. Thus jeopardized as the feudal Lord of Galloway, Fergus maintained the semi-independence of Galloway in several respects—legally, territorially, militarily, and ecclesiastically.

Fergus's son and heir Uchtred Lord of Galloway with his Cumbrian wife naturally promoted feudalism in Galloway, for which he lost his lordship and his life. But he was exonerated by his sons Roland Lord of Galloway and Duegald—the eponym of this family/clan, the MacDougalls of Gairachloyne and Lougan, with descendants, on the Irish Sea coast in the Rhinns of Galloway.

We are genetically Gaels in the male line but politically feudal, which means "land for military service." The old elected clan chiefs led their clansmen to acquire communal lands, whereas feudal leaders were granted by the Crown and inherited by male primogeniture their private ownership of lands, baronies, and territories. They received rent, goods, and services from their vassalage and reciprocated military and political support with the Crown.

The MacDougalls/Macdowalls of Galloway were ever loyal to the kings of Scotland with the sad exception of King Robert de Brus, the long Norman jealousy of whose family was anathema on Galloway. His feud (1306) for the kingship against the Baliols and Comyns in and of Galloway with most of their relations, allied us closely with the MacDougalls of Lorn and became a national civil war with international participation throughout his life.

Our lands and titles and archives were forfeited from us, and our survival became dependent on our Plantagenet cousins, the English Kings Edward I, II, and III, for three of our generations until 1413–4 when our original lands, with Garthland as well, were regranted to us. That was accomplished through Garthland's senior cadet (branch) in the barony of Makerstoun in Roxburghshire, as described in this book by their descendant, Bill MacDougall. The descents of the Houses of Gairochloyne and Logan, and Garthland and Freugh, and others will be described under separate cover, but the lands and edifices of the Galloways and Macdowalls are outlined here with thanks to Scott MacDougald and Walter Macdougall of the Clan MacDougall Society of North America.

Most significantly, the histories of some of the family diaspora in the United States and abroad are included to record new information on this ancient Scots name which had been spelled already in every conceivable way. The associated names are important, especially when the descent can be found, but it is the spirit that counts!

For this book I am grateful to the Officers of the Clan MacDougall Society of North America for their kind collaboration, to my fellow clansmen and co-authors for their successful pains, to Suzanne McDougal for her skillful copy and publishing expertise, and to my wife Alexandra for her patience and devoted computer work.

Fergus Macdowall
Editor-in-Chief
2009

The personal Coat of Arms of
Prof. Fergus Day Hort Macdowall of Garthland,
Baron of Garochloyne, Garthland, and Castlesemple,
Chief of the Name and Arms of MacDowall
Source: Lyon Court, Edinburgh

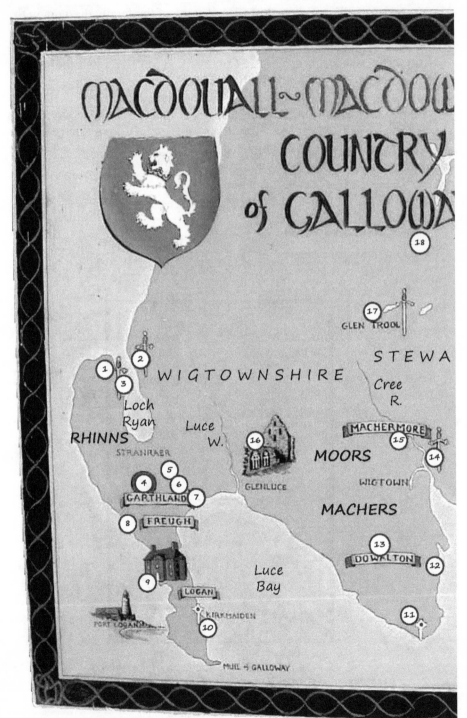

Legend on page xiv

ELL~MACDOWALL

Macdowall~MacDowell
Country of Galloway
Senior Descendants of the House
of Fergus, First of The Ancient
Lords of Galloway
⟸ Indicates Principal Branches
Off Map: MAKERSTON senior codes
of Garthland ~ on River Tweed
STODRIG McDowall of
Stodrig ~ close to Kelso

25
DUMFRIES 24

RTRY OF KIRKCUDBRIGHT
26
Urr   Nith
Dee   W.   R.
R.

T   23
20
21
Baronies (now Parishes)
granted to reconcile
Sir Duncan MacDowgall's family: K
Borgue (B), Twynholm (T),
Kelton (K) etc.
22
B
19
Wigtown   DUNDRENNAN
Bay

ISLE OF MAN
⬇ 27

Courtesy of Walter M. Macdougall, enhanced by Suzanne O. McDougal

Map Legend

1. **Corswall**—a Campbell Barony inherited by MacDowalls of Garthland in 1591.
2. **Glen App**—Where Alpin, King of the Scots, was killed in 741 on the east side of Loch Ryan after a flight from Northern Picts.
3. **Loch Ryan**—Where in 1307 Sir Dougal MacDougall of Gairochloyne (Garthland), Logan and Elrig defeated and captured Thomas and Alexander Bruce, two brothers of King Robert I (Bruce).
4. **Garthland Tower**—Seat of Macdowall of Garthland, 1413–1811. Built in 1211 and pulled down circa 1840.
5. **Saulseat Abbey**—Founded by Fergus Lord of Galloway in 1160.
6. **Stoneykirk Cemetery**—Burial place of Garthland and Freugh Macdowalls.
7. **Freugh**—Seat of M'Dowall of Freugh.
8. **Gairochloyne**—Original seat of Macdowall of Garthland.
9. **Logan House**—Seat of the MacDoualls of Logan, and now the location of a famous botanical garden.
10. **Kirkmaiden Cemetery**—Burial place of the MacDoualls of Logan.
11. **Whithorn Priory**—Founded by Fergus, Lord of Galloway. The nearby Candida Casa, founded by Ninian, Scotland's first saint, is on the isle of Whithorn.
12. **Cruggleton Castle**—Seaside fortification of the Lords of Galloway and the Norse before them.
13. **Dowalton**—Old seat of a branch of Garthland. Near Ravinstoun (with Longcastle) original seat of the Freugh family.
14. **Kirouchtrie**—Site of a decisive victory in 1308 by Edward Bruce over his opponents in Galloway.
15. **Machrimore Castle**—Seat of Macdowall of Machrimore.
16. **Glenluce Abbey**—Founded by Roland Lord of Galloway in 1190.
17. **Glen Trool**—Site of first victory of King Robert I (Bruce) over Baliol (Galloway–English) forces. Marked by Bruce's stone.
18. **Forest of Buchan**—Where John of Lorn, later the 5th Chief of Clan MacDougall, with Doual Macdowyl outflanked and almost captured King Robert I (Bruce).
19. **Palace Isle**—Castellated home of Fergus, Lord of Galloway, on an islet in the (now dry) Loch Fergus near Kirkcudbright.
20. **Threave Castle**—Seat of Archibald "the Grim" Lord of Galloway.
21. **Buittle (Botel) Castle**—Stronghold of the Lords of Galloway, Dervorgilla, and the Balliols.
22. **Isle of Heston**—Site of Sir Duncan Macdowall's stronghold, 1310–1353.
23. **Sweetheart Abbey**—Founded by Dervorgilla (Balliol), Lady of Galloway, in 1273.
24. **Dumfries**—Where Robert the Bruce murdered John Comyn in Greyfriars Kirk in February 1306. Dumfries Castle was starved into surrender by King Robert I (Bruce) while it was defended by Sir Dougal Macdougall/Macdowyl in 1313.
25. **Lincluden Abbey**—Founded circa 1161–65 by Uchtred, Lord of Galloway.
26. **Clatteringshaws Loch**—Site of battle in 1307 won by King Robert I (Bruce) against Galloway. Marked by Bruce's stone.
27. **Isle of Man**—Prince Fergus's daughter married the Norse King of Man and the Isles. Sir Dougal Macdowyl took and defended Man against King Robert I (Bruce) who invaded, captured, and banished Dougal in 1313. Sir John MacDougall of Lorn recaptured Man in 1315 but soon followed Dougal.

Ancient History of the MacDowalls

Fergus D. H. Macdowall and William L. MacDougall

It is scarcely 25 miles from Northern Ireland to Scotland's Galloway coast—a figurative stone's throw over the North Channel, which has been an overseas highway for Celts since long before the birth of Christ.

So, too, this cold and stormy arm of the Atlantic has served as the link between branches of one of the oldest named families of Gaelic ancestry, the MacDowalls, with a distinguished history dating back centuries.

Because records were lost, there is disagreement about the origin of the MacDowalls in Galloway. According to family legend, the Lords of Galloway were descended from Dovallus, a prince of Galloway in 230 B.C. Yet the historian P. H. M'Kerlie speculates that they descend from Somerled of Argyll, contrary to heraldic judgments made when some evidence was still available. Regardless, the belief of MacDowalls in their descent from the ancient House of Galloway would still be valid, though evidence for the early establishment of a MacDougall of Argyll in Galloway would be most illuminating.

Yet the most reasonable supposition is that the common ancestors of the MacDowalls and the MacDougalls appeared as leaders during the era when the Kingdom of Dalriada was being established in Scotland and when, according to the historian William Forbes Skene, an army of Galwegians helped Kenneth MacAlpin conquer the Picts.

Family Name and Ancestry

With roots leading back to an ancient age of warfare in the first millennium, the MacDowalls (also called MacDoualls, Macdowells, and the MakDougals of Makerstoun) boast a surname deriving from *Dughaill* (dark stranger). That name was used by the Gaels in referring to the Danes who invaded Ireland and Scotland over many decades. The MacDowalls share a variation of their name with the MacDougalls of Argyll, who may be distantly related; both families have long been associated with each other in peace and war.

In the MacDowall variation of *Dughaill*, the "h" aspirates the "g" to a sound like "w." This name became loosely associated with Galloway, where the Danes ruled from 875 to around 1000 A.D. While there is evidence in Irish records that this name was being used as a titled surname as early as 1162, it was not firmly established until the practice of such surnames came into general use at the end of the 13th century.

That *Dughaill* was the clan name of Fergus Lord of Galloway and his collaterals is considered by some historians to be reasonable and is supported by the historical tradition that the MacDowalls descend from this House of ancient Galloway.

The Highland MacDougalls' patronymic Dougall, King of Argyll and Lorn, was the oldest son of Somerled (King of Argyll, Kintyre, and of the South Isles) and his wife Ragnhildis. She was the daughter of King Olaf of Man and his second wife. Olaf's first wife was Affreca, the daughter of Fergus Lord of Galloway. Therefore, the MacDougalls of Lorn were connected with the House of Galloway in the female line.

The fact that Somerled and his MacDougall descendants share part of their blazon of arms (azure a lion rampart argent) with Fergus of Galloway and the MacDowalls is heraldic proof of direct and probably more ancient relationship. These arms are indicative of the Royal House of Lorn, that seaboard tribe of the Scottish kingdom of Dalriada which maintained its connection with the Irish for centuries and through which we, as MacDowalls and MacDougalls, may also descend from Godfrey mac Fergus of the ninth century. He was Lord of Airgialla (Oriel) and Lord of Innse Gall (the Western Isles), and father-in-law of Kenneth MacAlpin, the first king of all Scotland with roots in what is now County Derry, back to before the fifth century Dalriadic colonization of Scotland.

The ancestry of King (in Irish tradition) or Prince (in English) Fergus Lord of Galloway (born 1096, died 1161) is unknown today. But his Gaelic name, his Dalriadic arms, and his governing role in Galloway support the family belief that he inherited his office. We have presumed that his father was Malcolm, son of Earl Melkoff (Malcolm) who died in 1034 and was a native underlord in Galloway. Fergus's great-grandfather could have been Earl MacGill, who descended from the Earls of Innse Gall as did Somerled, and some mistakenly suggest that another Somerled was Fergus's father.

Fergus to Duncan

Galwegians of mixed origin constituted an independent principality that followed native leaders in the traditional Celtic manner, under the suzerainty of foreign earls or kings. Under King David I, Fergus was obliged to start replacing the Celtic tribal society of Galloway with Norman feudalism. Normans progressively married into native families of leadership throughout Scotland, and only in the remoteness of the Highlands did the clan system develop further.

Nevertheless, Galloway was for a long time wild and ambivalent toward both Scotland and England, and maintained its own jurisdiction for many centuries. The early royal charters of Scotland were addressed "To all good men, French, English, Scots and Galwegians."

Fergus lived chiefly on his Palace Isle in Loch Fergus, Kirkcudbright, and at Cruggleton Castle on the Solway cliffs near Wigtown. Under the leadership of David I, who founded eight abbeys throughout Scotland, Fergus founded in Galloway the abbeys of Saulseat, Tongland, and Dundrennan as well as the priories of Whithorn and Trayle (St. Mary's Isle). Fergus did not take Galloway to battle with Somerled in support of Somerled's brother-in-law, Malcolm MacHeth, but Fergus's complicity obliged him to take sanctuary as a monk in Holyrood Abbey.

The Tartan, Fall 1983

Artist's Reconstruction of Dundrennan Abbey

Fergus later expected support from Somerled when Fergus raised Galloway in revolt against Malcolm IV in an effort to place on the throne William of Egremont, the great-grandson of Malcolm Canmore and Ingibiorg of Galloway. When this effort failed, Fergus resigned his lordship and returned to Holyrood Abbey, where he died.

Fergus left two sons, Uchtred by his first wife, Elizabeth, youngest natural daughter of King Henry I of England, and Gilbert by his second, Celtic wife. By the Norse system of inheritance (clear proof that Fergus was not a Norman), Galloway was divided between Uchtred and Gilbert. The result was that the province was polarized east and west geographically, and Anglo-Norman and Celtic politically.

Uchtred founded Lincuden Abbey and other churches in the Norman tradition, and he married Gurnelda, daughter of Waldeve, Lord of

Allerdale, and brother of the second Earl of Dunbar. With Gurnelda, Uchtred had three recorded sons.

Uchtred and his brother Gilbert led the Galwegians who formed most of the Scots army of William the Lion against Henry II, but when William was captured at Alnwick in 1174, Gilbert aided and abetted a Galwegian backlash for independence.

Incredibly, Uchtred was murdered by Gilbert's son, Malcolm. Anglo-Normanism was eradicated in Galloway, and Gilbert usurped the lordship. Gilbert did homage to Henry II at York in 1175, together with the released William the Lion and Dougal son of Somerled. For his misdeeds, Gilbert paid a fine and left his elder son as a hostage of Henry for 10 years. In revenge, Gilbert was followed by Uchtred's son, Roland, who after a decade of exile in William's court emerged from Cumberland in 1185 with a friendly Norman baronage and became Lord of Galloway.

But the wings of Galloway were clipped forever in 1186 when William removed Nithsdale from the east of Galloway to establish the royal burgh of Dumfries. At the same time, Henry created the earldom of Carrick in the northwest, which Henry bestowed on Gilbert's son and heir, Duncan, in 1197.

Duegald to Robert the Bruce

This splendid array of ancient names still carried weight almost a millennium later. The McDoualls of Freugh claimed in about 1722 to be descended from Gilbert. Macdowall of Garthland claims descent from Roland's brother, Duegald, who was killed in 1185 while defeating a party of rebels in Galloway.

According to the Garthland "Greenbook," Duegald "is the root and stem of all the MacDowalls," and from this Duegald, also called Dunegal, his descendants were called MacDoualls, that is, the posterity of Donugall. The MacDoualls of Logan claimed descent from Thomas, natural son of Alan Lord of Galloway, from whom a Celtic patronym Mac-Dhu-Alan may have been derived.

Of further interest is the fact that Gilbert's son Duncan, Earl of Carrick, was succeeded by Niel, whose heiress Marjory brought the earldom to her second husband, Robert Bruce, Lord of Annandale. Their son, Robert Bruce, Earl of Carrick, who became King of Scotland, was a great-great-grandson of Fergus of Galloway, as was John Baliol (also spelled Balliol), King of Scotland, who was of the legitimate royal line to which Galloway was always faithful.

Roland, Lord of Galloway, had extensive holdings in England as well as in Scotland. These holdings contributed to the traditional ambivalence and independence of Galwegians, who helped to quell an insurrection against King Henry on the Welsh border in 1186. Roland also recovered Ross and Moray for King William in 1187. Roland married Elena, heiress of Richard de Morville, through whom he inherited in 1196 the office of Constable of Scotland. They had three sons and a daughter. Roland died in Northampton in 1200.

Roland's son Alan succeeded his father as Lord of Galloway and Constable of Scotland. As "Alan of Dunfres," he later became Chancellor of Scotland under King Alexander. Alan revived Galloway's sea power by building a large fleet, which ravaged the coast of Derry in 1212.

The fleet was commanded by Alan's brother Thomas, who became Earl of Athol by right of his wife, and Roderick son of Ronald of the Isles. In the same year, Alan led 1,000 Galwegians to assist King John of England in his invasion of Ireland. As a result, Irish Dalriada and the island of Rathlin were added to Alan's domains in Scotland and England.

Alan was one of the "Great barons of England" who in 1215 at Runnymede forced King John to sign the Magna Carta, to which the seal of our arms is attached. As a "Relative in the line of consanguinity," Alan attended the wedding of Henry III of England to Joanna, sister of King Alexander.

Alan had one daughter by his first wife, who may have been a daughter of Reginald of the Isles. Alan was later married to Margaret, eldest daughter of David, Earl of Huntingdon and brother of William the Lion. They had a son, Thomas, who died unmarried, and two daughters, the youngest of whom was Devorguilla.[*] Alan also had a natural son named Thomas, who married the daughter of Reginald, one of the rival kings of Man at the time.

Alan divided Galloway according to the Norman feudal laws of inheritance among his three surviving daughters, with his offices devolving on their Norman husbands. This break in the traditional Brehonic election of a male successor from the native governing family incensed the people of Galloway. While Alan's brother Thomas was overseas, King Alexander II refused to take over the lordship, so the people backed Alan's natural son Thomas to succeed Alan. Thomas had strong support from Ireland and the Isle of Man, under his wife's family, and he raised an insurrection that almost defeated King Alexander and his army in the wild country of Galloway in 1235.

Thomas eventually lost, but escaped, while Galloway suffered from the king's wrath. When Thomas returned the next year with another force from Ireland, the chastised Galwegians were unable to support him. The church helped "Thomas of Galloway" to throw himself on the mercies of

---

[*] Also spelled Devorgilla, Dervogilla, etc.

Alexander and Edward I, who kept Thomas and wife and son in custody for 50 years.

The office of Constable of Scotland was conveyed by Elena, daughter of Alan by his first marriage, to her locally unpopular Norman husband, Roger de Quincey. One of their daughters, Elizabeth, married Alexander Comyn (Cummin), Earl of Buchan, who became Constable of Scotland. The wealthiest man in Scotland, Alexander Comyn governed western Galloway as the first sheriff of Wigtownshire.

Alexander Comyn's brother married Marjory, the granddaughter of Alan of Galloway, and their daughter became the wife of Alexander MacDougall of Argyll, thus forming another close tie between the Houses of Lorn and Galloway.

Another daughter of Alan of Galloway, Christina, wife of the Earl of Albemarle, died in about 1246, which left her last surviving sister, Devorguilla, as Alan's sole heiress. Devorguilla's husband, John de Baliol, added the lordship of Galloway to his extensive territories in Scotland, England, and France.

Devorguilla, Lady of Galloway, endowed Balliol College, Oxford, which she and her husband founded. She also built the bridge over the Nith at Dumfries and founded Sweetheart (New) Abbey in 1273, where she was buried along with her husband's heart in 1290. Their son John survived three elder brothers to inherit the lordship of Galloway and successfully competed against Robert Bruce and the Black Comyn for the crown of Scotland in 1292. Marjory (Alianora), the third daughter of Devorguilla and sister of King John Baliol, married John, the Black Comyn of Badenoch, whose sister, as mentioned above, was the wife of Sir Alexander MacDougall of Argyll. In this way, our families—as the ancient Houses of Argyll and Galloway—were fatefully bound in common cause in 1306 before the act at the altar of Greyfriars Church, in Dumfries.

"I Will Go and Mak Siccar"

It was an act so despicable that many people in Scotland, the crowned heads of Europe, and the Pope were in agreement for once, out of sheer horror.

On February 10, 1306, Robert Bruce and John "the Red" Comyn of Badenoch, son of Marjory Baliol and John "the Black" Comyn, met at Greyfriars Church in Dumfries to discuss which of the two rivals should be the King of Scotland. Suddenly, the discussion turned violent and, before the high altar, Bruce stabbed Comyn. Comyn fell, bleeding, but was still alive.

Bruce moaned to his aides that he might have killed the Red Comyn. One of his vassals shouted, "I will go and mak siccar"—I will go and make certain—and ran to the altar, where he stabbed Comyn repeatedly, completing the murder.

Even in a world of that time when assassinations were not uncommon, this one—at the foot of an altar—was too much for many to take. The act was widely denounced by kings and commoners alike, and the Pope responded by excommunicating Bruce, an action with potentially crippling consequences for Bruce. King Edward of England prepared for war against the usurper.

But despite the furor, Robert Bruce achieved what he wanted. On March 25, 1306, he was proclaimed Robert I, King of Scotland.

Dougal Macdougall

At this turbulent time in history, the lineal descendant of Duegald of Galloway, brother of Roland Lord of Galloway, was Dougal Macdougall. In 1295, Dougal received a charter from John I, King of Scotland, confirming Dougal in "terras de Garochloyne, Lougan, Elrig, etc., in Wigtownshire." Garochloyne,* the old designation of the barony of Garthland, may be translated from the Gaelic as the "joyful, tufted mount."†

Today, the estate of Garthland Mains, which lies between Stranraer and Stoneykirk, belongs to the Earl of Stair. The Garthland Tower/Castle stood on that site from 1211 to 1812. It rose within its yard or garth and was probably surrounded by a wooden palisade in the Norman style.

The location was in strategic command of the isthmus of the Rhinns of Galloway with a full view of Loch Ryan toward Ailsa Craig in the north and of Luce Bay toward the Isle of Man in the south. The date stone from the battlements of Garthland Castle, which bears the date 1274 in Roman numerals, is in the possession of Fergus D. H. Macdowall, together with the actual site of the tower.

Both Dougal and his brother Fergus Macdougall of the county of Wigtown joined most of the baronage of Scotland at the parliament of the English king, Edward I, at Berwick. There they swore oaths of homage. Their names were transcribed in the "Ragman Roll" as Dougal MacDowyl and Fergus Macdowald.

The MacDowalls of Galloway, with blood ties to the English crown as well as to the Scottish crown, remained loyal to Edward, who took personal possession of the province after he deposed King John Baliol, father of the Red Comyn's wife.

Sir Alexander MacDougall of Argyll and his son, John of Lorn, also subscribed to the Ragman Roll but soon repudiated it. In fact, in his

---

* Also spelled Gairachloyne, Gairochloyne, etc.
† Garochloyne was originally named *Caerlachlan* or "Fort of the Norse."

continued lordship over the Western Isles at this time, bestowed by King John I, Alexander "MacDubgall" not only attacked Alexander of the Isles, who was allied to Edward I, but also killed Alexander MacDouell. The Irish Annals maintained that MacDouell was "One of the best of Ireland and Scotland."

Ten years later, however, the Comyn relationship of John of Lorn and Dougal of Gairochloyne made them the two most inveterate enemies of Robert the Bruce.

In February 1307, Dougal as Edward's sergeant in Galloway captured Robert Bruce's brothers, Thomas and Alexander, and Sir Reginald Crawford when they landed in Loch Ryan with a force of some 700 men from Ireland.

The captives were conveyed to King Edward at Carlisle, where they were executed. Dougal was knighted and his son was rewarded with the gift in marriage to a prominent heiress.

When Robert Bruce returned to his own Carrick coast from his refuge on the Island of Rathlin, he was forced into the security of the Galloway hills, where John of Lorn's men tracked him. Shortly afterwards Edward I died, and Robert devastated most of Galloway, but retired before the Earl of Richmond, Viceroy of Scotland, who was sent in at Macdowyl's's request.

Robert and Edward Bruce then gained support in the Highlands, where they defeated the Earl of Buchan, chief of the Comyns at that time. Then Robert attacked and wasted the district of Lorn, capturing Dunstaffnage castle in the process. Robert and Edward Bruce made a new and successful campaign against Galloway, for which Robert granted Edward the Lordship of Galloway. The critical battles were fought at the rivers Dee and Cree, and "M'Dowall" is said to have been slain while he was being pursued.

Another version states that Dougal MacDouall was forced by famine to surrender Dumfries castle to Robert Bruce in 1313. Still another story indicates that the same M'Dowall may have been slain when Robert subjugated the Isle of Man after ravaging Cumberland. The family then fought against Robert at Bannockburn (1314) where Sir Dougal's oldest son and heir Dougal was killed.

※ ※ ※

The early years of the Second Millennium were turbulent, yet the middle years were to be even more troubled.

Troubled Years

Fergus D. H. Macdowall and William L. MacDougall

Wars, fires, and the ravages of time have taken their toll on the records of the MacDowalls, but enough primary and secondary sources of information are left to paint an intriguing picture of how the kinsmen fared in the turbulent middle years of the Second Millennium.

For a while, it appeared that virtually no documents would survive the turmoil. After many decades of violence that affected almost all families in Scotland and Ireland, the records that might have survived into the 15th century were entirely rifled and confiscated by Sir Archibald Douglas when he obtained the Lordship of Galloway from Scotland's King David II.

Douglas forced all vassals of the crown to give up the charters and evidence of their estates and tenements which he planned to hold. If any of them held back, the houses of the offenders were utterly destroyed, and all charters by which they held their possessions were irrecoverably lost.

This is why neither the house of Garthland nor any other of the ancient families in Galloway have any writs preceding the reign of Robert III, who died in 1406. The destruction of the abbeys during the Reformation and accidental house fires gave the coup de grace to surviving collections. These included McDouall of Logan's seat, Balzieland, which was destroyed by fire in about 1500.

McDouall of Freugh's house and castle were gutted in 1650 and 1680, and Garthland's surviving records, including evidence of their charter of 1295, were lost in the accidental burning of Preston Hall in Edinburgh in 1686. The charter was copied obscurely in old Saxon on a copper plate that had survived four centuries mounted in the parish church of Stoneykirk (St. Stephen's Church) near Garthland.

From the last record in 1313 of the recipient of this charter, Dougal MacDougall (Macdowylt) of Gairochloyne, to the bequeathing of the same properties to Thomas McDowyll in 1413, one has to rely on the recorded witnessing of other papers to piece together the succession of this House. Historian M'Kerlie cites convincing documentation that in the interim, Dougal was succeeded by "Duncano Magdowell" who held out precariously on Eastholm (now Heston), the most eastern islet off the Kirkcudbright coast.

Duncan's allegiance to David II was enforced by Thomas Randolph, Earl of Moray, and Archibald Douglas when they wasted Galloway in 1332 pursuing Edward Baliol. Duncan switched sides in 1339 to support another comeback of Edward Baliol to the crown, and when opposed by Malcolm Fleming, Earl of Wigton, he obtained aid by sea from King Edward III of England, including "ten tuns [casks] of wine" in 1342.

The continuity of support from Dougal to Duncan by the first three Edwards of England is good evidence of Duncan's succession to Dougal as head of the family and public leader in Galloway. In 1347, however, Duncan and his oldest son fought for David II and Scotland in the Battle of Neville's Cross at Durham, where they were captured with King David. They were held in the Castles of Rochester and York until Duncan was exchanged for his wife and brother as hostages. After a year, in the face of the Black Death advancing north from England, he obtained their exchange for others and for his help to resettle Baliol in Galloway.

In 1353, however, Sir William, first Earl of Douglas, reduced Galloway and compelled Duncan to swear allegiance before the Regent of Scotland (Stewart) at Cumnock, Ayrshire.

The name "Duncan" as the son and heir of Dougal MacDougall of Garochloyne is interesting in that Duncan of Argyll succeeded the first Dougal MacDougall of Argyll, 108 years before. Duncan MacDougall of Dunollie, friend of the rebel William Wallace, succeeded his nephew, John of Lorn, as Chief of the Highland MacDougalls at about the same time in 1320 that Duncan MacDougall succeeded to our House in Galloway.

The historian M'Kerlie found that Duncan had three sons with his first wife: Duncan, Dowgall (Dougal), and John; that this Dougal succeeded his father; and that Sir Fergus MacDougall of Makerstoun was Duncan's son by his second wife, Margaret Fraser, heiress of Makerstoun. Alternatively, the Garthland Manuscripts surmised that Dougal succeeded the Dougal of the Ragman Roll and that his sons were Sir Fergus, his heir, and Dougal who married Margaret Fraser and begat Fergus MacDougall of Makerstoun. However, all dates favor M'Kerlie's account.

Dougal had extensive grants of land from King David II in Kirkcudbright and undoubtedly also in the County of Wigtown, where he was Sheriff of Wigtown in 1361. The surname of this generation was variously spelled in charters as Macdougall, Mcdowgall, M'dowalle, Mcdowyll, Macdowall, etc. In his day the ambitious bastard Sir Archibald "the Grim" or "the Black" Douglas obtained rule of Kirkcudbright from David II in 1369 and achieved the entire Lordship of Galloway after continued pressures of the Macdowalls and McCullochs against the Flemings forced Thomas Fleming to give up his Earldom of Wigtown to Douglas in 1372.

The Black Douglas quartered the Galloway Lion with the Douglas arms and took up residence in Prince Fergus's Palace Isle in Loch Fergus until his dreaded Threave Castle was built. Sir Fergus Macdowyl, who was knighted by David II, attached himself to Douglas and was made sheriff-depute for the Constabulary of Kirkcudbright.

Threatening imprisonment and death, the despotic Archibald required that all landowners should deliver up all charters with the unkept promise of granting his own in their place. On this pretext he expelled Agnew, hereditary Sheriff of Wigtown, and blew up his King's Castle of Lochnaw in about 1390. When in 1385 the Black Douglas amended the code of Galloway in Parliament, the MacDowalls helped assure that some of its ancient statutes were maintained, with the result that the general law of Scotland was not applied to Galloway until 1426.

In 1388, the second Earl of Douglas died at his famously won Battle of Otterburn against the English, and was succeeded by Archibald, Lord of Galloway, who died the most powerful subject of the King in 1400.

Sir Fergus was comrade-in-arms of Archibald's son and heir, Archibald, fourth Earl of Douglas, Lord of Galloway. When they were returning from a raid in England in 1402, they were met by Percy (Hotspur) Earl of Northumberland and the renegade Earl of March at the Battle of Homildon Hill. The Scottish forces were decimated by archery, and few of the flower of all Scotland's chivalry survived.

Among the survivors were Archibald, Earl of Douglas, and Sir Fergus, who were wounded, captured, and briefly held to ransom. Sir Fergus succeeded his mother in the Barony of Macarstoun (Makerstoun) in Teviotdale, Roxburghshire, by charter in the rolls of Robert II, of 1373. His sons were Sir Dungal and Uchtred, who were in records before the century closed.

There were three successive Dungal Makdowells of Makerstoun and a grandson Patrick McDougall, one of whose sons, Robert, emigrated to Sweden. He was the ancestor of Col. Gustavus and his son, Col. Alexander McDougall, Barons of Lodvica from 1674. From Makerstoun Parish also descended a Professor William Macdowell in the Netherlands three centuries ago. The Makdougalls of Makerstoun ended in the male line with Sir Henry Hay-Makdougall of Makerstoun, whose daughter's husband, Gen. Sir Thomas Brisbane, also assumed the name Makdougall in 1826. Brisbane, Australia, was named after him.

Garthland history returned to a sure footing when, in 1413, "Sir Fergusio McDowyll" witnessed a charter from Archibald, fourth Earl of Douglas, which reinstated the original family barony Garochloyne under Fergus's elder brother's son, Thomas. At that time, King James I was still a captive in England, but in 1426 Thomas was styled "Thomas Macdouall de Garflane" when he witnessed a charter under the great seal of James I. Thomas MacDowall of Garthland died in about 1440, leaving several sons, including his heir, Uchtred.

Uchtred Macdowall, his heir Thomas, and their successors were styled of Garochloyne or of Garthland, and in Uchtred's time, Logan and Freugh—properly Freuch—first appeared as separate family baronies. One writ shows that Uchtred Macdowall of Garthland obtained Elrig and other lands from Patrick MacDouall of Logan and disponed them to a younger brother, Andrew. This may indicate that either this Patrick or his father Patrick was Uchtred's younger brother, who inherited Logan and Elrig from their father, Thomas MacDowall of Garthland, Logan, and Elrig. This also supplies a basis for Logan's belief, two centuries later, that they descended from Thomas of Galloway.

Yet another brother of Uchtred was Gilbert, initially of Barjarg, the lands of which were an early possession of the McDoualls of Freugh. The first on the Freugh record was Gilbert McDouall of Ravinstoun, whose son Gilbert received the lands of Urril upon his marriage in 1445. Later his lands included Ravinstoun and Freugh and the patronage of the church of Stoneykirk by crown charter. Garthland considers it a strong presumption that the first listed Gilberts (Barjarg and Ravinstoun) were the same person, and this also serves to support Freugh's understanding that the initial progenitor of their line was of the name Gilbert of Galloway.

In 1445, all three families were witnesses to the investment of Andrew Agnew as heir to his father in properties and the office of hereditary sheriff. The representatives in order of registration were: Thomas M'Dowall, who was the younger of Garthland, Gilbert M'Dowall of Freugh, and Patrick M'Dowall of Logan. When Andrew M'Dowall of Elrig was sheriff-depute in 1484, many of the name witnessed a writ to Quentin Agnew, third hereditary sheriff. These included Uchtred M'Dowall of Garthland, Andrew M'Dowall of Myroch, Uchtred M'Dowall of Dalreagle, and Uchtred M'Dowall of Mindork.

Galloway families were victorious in the Battle of Sauchieburn against James III, fought on the Stirling plain in 1488, which brought the crown to the Prince Royal. Local feuds and lawlessness flourished in Galloway as in the Highlands, and in 1494, Uchtred Macdowall of Garthland, grandson of Uchtred, son of Thomas, was appointed a sheriff-depute.

Balzieland, the seat of the second-known Patrick McDouall of Logan, was destroyed together with family records by an accidental fire in 1500. Six years later, James IV made a pilgrimage on foot to the Shrine of St. Ninian at Whithorn, Galloway, to which he ascribed the recovery to good health of his Queen Margaret. They returned in thanksgiving and, as an example of their representation of the ancient indigenous families of Galloway, Uchtred Macdowall of Garthland and Sir Alexander McCulloch of Myrtoun carried the Host before the royal couple in the church procession at Whithorn.

Seven years later, this popular and chivalrous King accepted an appeal from Louis XII and the challenge of his Queen of France and led the largest Scottish army ever assembled against England. The ensuing Battle of Flodden was lost, together with the lives of James IV and the flower of Scotland's nobility. A still higher proportion of the Galloway baronage was lost, including Uchtred Macdowall of Garthland and his son Thomas, Charles McDouall of Logan, Gilbert McDouall of Freugh, and most of their male relations.

The successor of Freugh, Fergus McDouall, appears to have been a man of violence. He and John Macdowall of Garthland and Corswall, grandson of Thomas who was killed at Flodden, were killed at Pinkie in 1547. That battle was lost to the Duke of Somerset who, as Regent for English King Edward VI, invaded Scotland to obtain obedience just after King Henry VIII died. We can speculate that the MacDowalls were among the Earl of Home's lightly armed horsemen long characteristic of Galloway arms.

The three families were united in the next generation when John's daughter Helen married Patrick McDouall of Logan and daughter Florence married James McDouall of Freugh. John's son and heir, Uchtred Macdowall of Garthland, was highly esteemed at the Court and in the country, and he championed the family of which he was universally reputed Chief. There was already old Lochinvar blood in the family, but as protector of his kindred, Uchtred entered a long, expensive and sanguine feud against the bellicose Gordons of Lochinvar after one of theirs killed Gilbert MacDouall of Barjarg—at this time a cadet branch of the McDoualls of Freugh.

Those were the days of Sir John Gordon of Lochinvar of border romance, and Garthland was involved in a story that might have been the model for a popular ballad by Sir Walter Scott.

Struggles

Fergus D. H. Macdowall and William L. MacDougall

The MacDowalls were touched lightly in the turbulent years of the religious Reformation and Counter-Reformation. Court intrigues, murder and a rebellious nobility raged about Mary Queen of Scots and her young son who became James VI of Scotland and I of England.

In that period, Uchtred Macdowall of Garthland married his second wife, Margaret, daughter of Henry, Lord Methven, whose sister was the Countess of Gowrie.

As a result, Uchtred and his son and heir, Uchtred, took part in the attempt of Alexander Ruthven, Earl of Gowrie, to separate the young King James VI from his advisers, who were influencing him to return to Catholicism in 1584. They seized the king and the castle and town of Stirling but were overpowered and convicted.

The Earls of Gowrie, Angus, and Mar and all but three of their retainers were hanged, drawn, and quartered. Two of the three who were spared were our two Uchtreds. The elder Uchtred found it politic to end his years "in France." The younger, who was a "man of great esteem," agreed to settlements of disputes with the result that his only son, in 1590, married Janet Gordon of Lochinvar, our former adversaries.

In 1598, this younger Uchtred defended some lands he held from the Earl of Cassilis (Kennedy), high treasurer, who with 40 horsemen sought to repossess them. With 100 fully equipped men at arms and fellow barons, the Laird of Garthland besieged the Earl on his isle on Loch Inch, Wigtownshire, until the terms of law were agreed. Uchtred died two years later.

Another family allied in the heraldic arms of MacDowall that existed in the 16th Century and persisted for at least 200 years were the Macdowells of Stodrig (Stotharige) in Teviotdale, to the east in the Shire of Roxburgh. This branch started with Thomas McDowall, a burgess of Edinburgh who bought the land and obtained a charter in 1520. Stodrige House was built in 1593.

The Lordship of Galloway had been held by the crown since it was forfeited from the Earl of Douglas in 1455. In 1613, when Sir John Macdowall of Garthland, grandson of our last Uchtred, was at the Court of James VI, Sir John rivaled his brother-in-law Sir Alexander Stewart, Baron Garlies, for the Lordship of Galloway on the grounds of his heirship in lineal descent. However, Sir John's patron, Sir John Ker, Earl of Somerset, lost favor on conviction of murder, and Lord Garlies was elevated to the Earldom of Galloway by the interest of his kinsman, the

Duke of Lennox. Fourteen years later, Sir John Macdowall and the Sheriff Sir Patrick Agnew were elected by fellow barons of Wigtownshire to negotiate with the King's Commissioners for the surrender of their tithes to Charles I.

Sir John was one of five commissioners selected in the Western Counties in 1634 for Charles's High Commission Court for the Scottish Episcopal Church, but he died in 1637. The most important consequence of the Court was the foundation of the Presbyterian Solemn League and Covenant in reaction against it. Galloway was the cradle of the Covenant as well as of the Reformation, and a strong Galloway force was in the Presbyterian army that took Newcastle in 1639. Sir John's successor Sir James Macdowall was appointed by the Estates as Commissioner of Supply and then a member of the Wigtownshire Committee of War, together with Alexander McDouall of Logan, Uchtred McDouall of Freugh, and others, to raise men to suppress the rebellion in Ireland.

Sir James was given command of the horse of Wigtown, represented the barons at the Convention of Estates in 1643, and was elected to the third Parliament of Charles I in 1644. Other MacDowalls on the War Committees over a five-year period were Hugh McDowall of Knockglass, Alexander MacDowall of Killeser, Alexander McDowall of Leffnoll, and MacDowall of Dalreagle. The first three of these were all cadets of Garthland.

The Galloway regiment of dragoons in the Parliament's army defeated the Royalists at Philiphaugh in 1645. But the Scotch Estates were also violently opposed to Cromwell's republican English Independents. John McDouall of Freugh, however, was a high Royalist in support of Charles I. He fought English forces in Galloway, was captured and taken to England, then escaped, but his house (Balgreggan) and fort (Castle McDouall) at Freugh were burned.

Sir James Macdowall of Garthland went to Ireland in 1647 to arrange to bring back the Scots army detachment there to relieve Charles I in England, and he was knighted by the king when Charles put himself into the hands of the Scots army outside Newark. Charles was executed in England in 1649 and Cromwell invaded Scotland in 1650. Three years later, Sir James was elected to advise Cromwell in London of the formal submission of the Galloway barons. Uchtred McDouall of Freugh, like his father John, was a firm Royalist and had military commands in Scotland and Ireland. After the Restoration, he was chosen a member of the first Parliament in 1661 called by Charles II.

The roughness of the times became apparent again at the end of 1660. Alexander McDouall of Logan was killed when, as the guardian of the heiress of Gordon of Clanyard, he overtook her abductors, the

Gordons of Kenmure, and rescued her after 40 men were killed. Patrick younger of Logan pursued and hanged the Gordon leader.

In 1677, the Council ordered the appointment of John Graham of Claverhouse, pronounced "Clavers," as one of the deputy sheriffs in Carrick and Wigtownshire. Graham was later known as "Bonnie Dundee" and won the battle of Killiekrankie, where he died in 1689.

The deputy sheriffs enforced the laws against Presbyterian Covenanters by killing people who gathered to pray independently of the prescribed Church.

Graham's army of dragoons and 6,000 Highland foot soldiers terrorized the country, pillaged the dwellings and castles, and carried off or destroyed all family heirlooms. Patrick McDouall of Freugh, Uchtred's heir, helped to lead a rising in protest. After the action at Bothwell Bridge, he was sentenced to be executed, but was not caught. As a result, Claverhouse acquired the Barony and title of Freugh in 1683.

Sir James Macdowall's heir, William Macdowall of Garthland, was one of the last to hold out against taking the "Test" for the Episcopal branch of church that employed bishops, but he agreed under peer pressure when Garthland Castle was about to be leveled. The next year he was commissioner of supply for Wigtownshire, and in 1689 he was elected to the Grand Convention of Estates summoned by the Prince of Orange. He was a member of the First Parliament of William and Mary until his death in 1700. He loaned the surviving records of Garthland to Sir George MacKenzie, Lord Advocate to Charles II and James VII. Later his house, Preston Hall, and all records went up in smoke.

The lands of Freugh were recovered in 1691–3 for Patrick, the son of Patrick McDouall, but the exact arms that were destroyed were no longer known. At this time, Logan House was the seat of Patrick McDouall of Logan who registered his arms in the Lord Lyon's office.

Patrick McDouall of Freugh was succeeded by his son, John, who entered his family into the peerage through his marriage in 1725 to Lady Elizabeth Dalrymple Crichton, heiress of the Countess of Dumfries. As a result, their son, Patrick McDouall Crichton, became in 1768 the sixth Earl of Dumfries. He ended the connection of his line with the caput baroniae (head barony) of Freugh when his only child, Elizabeth Penelope, married John Lord Mount Stuart.

Of their family, the oldest son, John, inherited both the Earldom of Dumfries and the Marquessate and Earldom of Bute. Many McDoualls, now chiefly in England, New Zealand, and Australia, are descended from John, the younger brother of Patrick sixth Earl of Dumfries, and are listed as collaterals of the House of Bute. They are now headed by Sir John Crichton-Stuart, sixth Marquess, eleventh Baronet (of Nova Scotia), Earl of Windsor, Viscount Mountjoy, Baron Mount Stuart, Baron

Cardiff, Earl of Dumfries, Viscount of Air, Lord Crichton, Earl of Bute, Viscount Kingarth, Lord Mountstuart, Cumrae and Inchmarnock; but he does not use the name or arms of McDouall of Freugh.

Robert McDouall of Logan had three sons: John, later of Logan; Andrew Lord Bankton, a Lord of Session and an outstanding lawyer; and Patrick of Culgroat. John's heir, Col. Andrew McDouall of Logan, was a member of Parliament for the County of Wigtown. He was succeeded in 1834 by his elder son, Col. (of the Life Guards) James McDouall of Logan. His successor, James, married Agnes, eldest daughter of Sir Thomas Buchan-Hepburn, of Smeaton Hepburn. They had three children: Andrew, Nigel, and Helen. Andrew and Nigel were country gentlemen and developed their well-known botanical gardens at Logan. Regrettably, they died unmarried and without children, and are buried beneath a tombstone inscribed "The last of the McDoualls."

Helen became Marchioness of Ailsa (Kennedy), and Logan House became the seat of their first cousin once removed, Sir Ninian Buchan-Hepburn, M.P.

Col. William Macdowall of Castlesemple was born the fifth son of William of Garthland, acquired sugar plantations in the West Indies, moved the British sugar trade from Bristol to Glasgow, and purchased the barony of Hugh, eleventh Lord Semple, among other lands in Renfrewshire, in 1727. In the uprising of 1745, Prince Charles Edward Stewart—Bonnie Prince Charlie—retired north with his army through Glasgow, where he stayed at Colonel William's town house, "Shawfield Mansion," in the West Port. There he met Clementina Walkinshaw, by whom he sired the Duchess of Albany.

Mrs. Jean MacDougall Hadfield had correspondence between Garthland and the MacDougalls of Dunollie during those difficult years of 1715–1747 regarding the schooling of Alexander MacDougall (Alastair Dubh), twenty-third of Dunollie, and more particularly of his brother, Allan, who later became manager of the estates of Col. William Macdowall of Castlesemple on the Island of St. Kitts, West Indies.

In 1772, Garthland reverted to Colonel William's oldest son, William Macdowall, second of Castlesemple and member of Parliament. He was the subject of the popular Scottish ballad, "Willie's on to Melville Castle." He co-founded the first bank in Glasgow. In the third generation of the family at Castlesemple House, the West Indian sugar trade collapsed from debts that stemmed from the American Revolution and incursions by French naval forces, and by 1810 it was necessary to liquidate all family possessions, including the lands of Garthland.

Many family members died in that year, including the next William Macdowall of Garthland and Castlesemple, a longstanding member of Parliament in Pitt's Parliaments and King's Lieutenant for Renfrewshire;

James Macdowall, Provost of Glasgow; Gen. Hay Macdowall, who defeated the Dutch in Ceylon and was commander-in-chief in India at Madras; and the author's ancestor, Col. Day Hort Macdowall, who earlier had a civil service career in Bengal.

Another one of these brothers, Capt. David Macdowall Grant of Arndilly, had the satisfaction in 1782 of serving as midshipman under Admiral Rodney in the defeat of the French fleet at the Battle of the Saints, West Indies, which won British supremacy of the seas. His son was the first outstanding evangelist of Britain.

Successive nephews of William Macdowall of Garthland and third of Castlesemple acquired the estates of Barr and Garpel, which were part of the Castlesemple holdings at Lochwinnoch, as the substitute Garthland in Renfrewshire. Day Hort's second grandson, Capt. Day Hort Macdowall, emigrated from Garthland to Canada, where he became a member of the Northwest Council in 1883–5, representing the District of Lorne. He was elected the first member of Parliament for Prince Albert, Saskatchewan, in 1887, and he finally settled in Victoria, B.C. He inherited Garthland from his brother, and the author is his only grandson.

As it was necessary to dispose of Garthland House, Renfrewshire, in 1935, the remaining nucleus of the estate is Barr Castle, the 16th Century seat of Glen of Barr.

Within the family at large, McDowells are preponderant. It is evident that the spelling of the name was never consistent, but the consensus is that the use of "e" as the last vowel is an Irish influence. In 1984, in southwest Scotland, telephones were listed for 100 McDowalls and 13 McDowells, but in Northern Ireland there were listed six McDowalls and 400 McDowells.

In about 1850, there was a McDowel of Ballywillhill, County Down, Ireland, and of Gillespie, Wigtownshire, Scotland, whose name issued from Garthland. These alternate spellings are equally balanced in the Highlands and in England, but in North America, McDowells predominate.

The channel between Galloway and Ireland was always a highway of travel, commerce, and invasion. Some settlement by the family in Ireland during the Plantation of Ulster—in about 1609—and in service of the Crown are likely possibilities for causing the differences in spelling. Interestingly, the common pronunciation of "Dow" is as read, but the Irish pronounce it "Doh" and the Garthland pronunciation is "Doo" in agreement with Logan, Freugh, and all MacDougalls.

Much work has to be done to uncover and accumulate more data on the connections and lines of descent of the MacDowalls of Galloway over the past millennium, including their migrations abroad. For that purpose, the editors of this book hope to learn about other aspects of the family and include that material in a future edition. We hope that many will contribute questions and family trees and that MacDowalls and MacDougalls in general will discover and add pertinent information. As Madam Coline MacDougall of MacDougall said, "The important thing is keeping the family ties!"

Makdougals of Makerstoun

Fergus D. H. Macdowall and William L. MacDougall

Nearly a thousand years ago, a small tower to repel attacks by the English was built on a hill overlooking the Tweed River along the southern border of Scotland. The tower was at the center of an estate called Makerstoun (pronounced Mak-AIR-ston), long a home of Norman feudal barons.

By standards of that time, when most of Scotland was poor and isolated, Makerstoun and its neighboring areas were prosperous. Farmers raised abundant cattle and sheep, woolens were exported all over Europe, and trade flowed over a network of old Roman roads to trading centers and ports. The estate is still one of the premier properties in Roxburghshire, graced with picturesque barns and a white mansion, Makerstoun House.

Painting by Robert Frain, ca. 1840; black/white photo courtesy of
The Rt. Hon. Mary Lady Biddulph, through Fergus D.H. Macdowall

"Rob o' the Trows," boatman to Gen. Sir Thomas Brisbane-Makdougal,
on the Tweed River with the old tower of Makerstoun behind

The Barony of Makerstoun is the most easterly portion of ancient Macdowall lands, 115 miles east of Garthland and two miles north of the remains of the ancient castle of Roxburgh, three miles west of Kelso and 30 miles south of Edinburgh.

An old tradition has it that some Macdowalls first moved to the Makerstoun area from Galloway as early as 1230 (about the same time, for comparison, as the Sixth Crusade in the Holy Land). However, it was in the 14th century that the first Macdowall became Baron of Makerstoun. Sir Fergus Macdowyll,* youngest son of Duncan Macdowyll, inherited the estate from his mother, Margaret Fraser. He also inherited two nearby properties, Yetholm and Clifton.

The estate became home to the Macdowells/Makdougalls of Makerstoun, who held the lands for five centuries and took their appanage (revenue for their maintenance) from the estate. Their descendants and the descendants of kinsmen they hired as farm workers, probably from Galloway, now number in the thousands. They are located not only in the Borders of Scotland but also across much of the world, including the United States, Canada, the Netherlands, Sweden, Estonia, Latvia, Germany, Russia, and Australia.

Evolution of the Makerstoun Family Name

Macdowyll—The recorded family surname first appeared as Macdowyll, which was the Anglo-Norman form in which Dougall Macdougall and his brother signed the Ragman Roll of King Edward I in 1296 to distinguish the Galloway family from the MacDougalls of Argyll. The colloquially spelled Macdowell (with Macdowel and Macdowal included) appeared early and persisted through nine generations within two centuries at Makerstoun.

Macdougal—Then Thomas Macdowell and his wife Margaret Hume, with an eye and ear to history in the 16th century, brought in the independent spelling of Macdougal, used by their successors for four generations.

Makdougal—Henry Macdougal and his wife Ann Scott (of Gala) named their children Makdougal as their own distinction, when the "k" was fashionable in the Lowlands, and this was maintained for three generations at Makerstoun.

Makdougal-Hay/Brisbane/Scott—Thomas Macdougal and his younger brother William, a merchant in Edinburgh, granted a discharge

---

* Recorded in a Latin charter as "Sir Fergusio Macdowyll." This branch of the MacDowalls was variously spelled MacDowyll, Macdowell, Macdougall, Makdougall, Mcdougall, Mcdowgall, Macdoual, etc., sometimes depending on the whim of clerks who recorded official papers in Roman script.

of their own claims to Makerstoun on July 27, 1715, in favor of their niece Barbara, the only remaining child of their oldest brother Henry Macdougal of Makerstoun and his wife, Ann Scott. Through Barbara and two more successive heiresses the family and surname merged with Hay (of Alderstone), Brisbane (of Brisbane), and Scott (of Gala). A Scott of Gala eventually sold the Barony of Makerstoun and dropped the Makdougal name in about 1935.

The present Macdougal heir presumptive could be the senior male heir in the direct line from either Thomas or William Macdougal (brothers of Henry 15th of Makerstoun in 1742) or the von Wahl family from six generations prior to them.

From Galloway, Not the Highlands

The lairds of Makerstoun, like Garthland, consistently used the lower case "d" unlike public scribes accustomed to Highland usage. They also claimed to be "a separate race" from the Highland MacDougalls, yet their spellings later edged toward conformity with the Gaelic derivation *Mac Dubh Ghael* (or *Gall*), "Son of the Dark Stranger," as the Gaels called the Danish Vikings.

This later return in Makerstoun to their ancient Macdougall patronymic in Galloway, combined with the Logan and later Freuch usage of "McDouall" there, induced some historians to hold that the Lowland MacDowalls are part of the Highland Clan MacDougall. The 18th century historian Nisbet said, "I am of the opinion that the McDouals of McCorston [Makerstoun] are descended from MackDougall or McCoul, the ancient Lords of Lorne." Another writer, Grace A. Elliot, stated, "From the ancient Lords of Galloway, princes in their own right and sphere, descended Kings of Scotland, and also the Makdougalls [of Makerstoun]."

The Makerstoun family history was written about 1830 by Anna-Maria Macdougal-Hay of Makerstoun and her husband, Gen. Sir Thomas Brisbane. They wrote:

> The tradition and belief have long prevailed that the MACDOWALS (for the "MACDOUGALS of MAKERSTON" seem of the same stock, and formerly spelt their surname in the same manner) are descended from the old Lords or Princes of Galloway, who were almost sovereigns in their own districts, although acknowledging fealty to the crown of Scotland. Occasionally all the Macdowals substituted "Macdougal" for "Macdowal", but the latter is by far the more prevalent, and appears the more correct orthography, and may possibly have been preferred in distinction from the "Macdougals" of the Highlands, who are a perfectly separate race.

An associated genealogical table (family tree) written by William Fraser in 1840 is in the British Museum, with slightly different information.

Thus, both the MacDougall and Macdowall names evolved from the Lorn heritage in the Western Isles, perhaps independently of the Galloway heritage. Yet until proof is shown that Sir Dougal Macdowyl of Gairachloyne was also of Lorn, the ancient Galloway heritage of the Macdowalls is generally accepted.

Arms

"The arms of the family of M'Dougall of Makerston, as in Pont's Manuscript, are azure, a lion rampant argent, crowned or, with a star of the first on the lion's shoulder" (Nisbet). Those arms would have been granted to or matriculated by Sir Fergus long before Nisbet published in about 1800. They are the arms of Garthland with an added star (Mullet) (blue) as a mark of cadency (a cadet branch) to represent the third surviving son, which Fergus was of Sir Duncan Macdowyll of forfeited Garochloyne.

In perhaps the latest mid-18th century matriculation, the arms of Makdougal of Makerstoun are quartered with those of Hay, and contain a plain lion rampant with an ermine escutcheon within bordure containing eight cinquefoils (strawberry flowers, from Fraser).

In both cases, the shields bearing the arms are not held by supporters; and the crests, a crowned demi-lion regardant, are differenced from that of M'Douall of Logan by the dexter (left) paw holding a cross-crosslet fitchee, which cants to the Highland MacDougalls.[*] Their motto "Fear God" was proudly carried as their identity to North America by their McDowell emigrants.

Sir Fergus

The first Macdowall baron of the feudal Barony of Makerstoun was identified in mid-14th century charters as "Sir Fergusio Macdowyll." He was the fourth and youngest son of Sir Duncan Macdowyll of Eastholm (now Heston) Island in the shire (now "Stewartry") of Kirkcudbright.

Sir Fergus was the only son and heir of Sir Duncan's second wife, Margaret Fraser of Makerstoun. She was the heiress of Sir Gilbert Fraser and his wife, Margaret Corbet, Anglo-Norman families from Teviotdale. The Frasers were originally from Anjou in France and possibly came to Scotland under King David I, as they appear in history in 1164 under King Malcolm IV. They were supporters of the Comyns in Scotland until

---

[*] This refers to three small crosses incorporated into one large cross, as seen in the Arms and badge of the Highland MacDougalls.

disaffection with King Edward I of England led them to side with Robert the Bruce in 1306 and to champion his cause for the crown of Scotland on the same side as the Douglases. George Crawford, the distinguished antiquarian and author of the Garthland manuscript of circa 1730, wrote:

> This Sir Fergus Macdowall of Garthland was the first of the family that seems to have lived in any kind of decency with the house of Douglas.

Crawford followed Balfour in writing that Sir Fergus was "of Garthland," which was repeated in Sir Andrew Agnew's "History of Galloway" in 1864. Since then it has been insistently reiterated by all others, including "Burke's Landed Gentry." In fact, Sir Fergus was indeed of the house of Garochloyne/Garthland, but he inherited his own cadet stirps (branch) of Makerstoun. He also assured his nephew's rightful inheritance of the senior line in Garthland.

Little else is known about Sir Fergus beyond his parentage, the dates of his succession to Makerstoun and of his investiture to knighthood (both in 1373), his capture at the battle of Homildon Hill on September 14, 1402, and his descendants.

To judge from the approximate time of his parents' marriage, Sir Fergus was at most 20½ years old in 1353 when his father's fort on the island of Eastholm was besieged across its causeway at low tide.

The attackers were a strong force under Sir William, Lord of Douglas (later their first Earl). He was acting in his role of Warden of the Marches of the border with England and as Brucean owner of Buittle Castle since 1324. His natural (bastard) uncle Sir Archibald "the Grim" was with him. Sir William descended on and evicted King Edward Baliol at Buittle Castle, and compelled many important Baliolites, including Sir Duncan Macdowall and probably his sons, to swear an oath of allegiance to King David II. The oaths took place in the church of Cumnock in Ayrshire, before the Regent Stewart (later King Robert II). At this time, western Galloway reverted to King David II of Scotland, who was in captivity in England.

For the next century (1355–1455), the Douglases were the most powerful family in Scotland. Sir William was the lineal heir and grandson of Sir James "the Good" Douglas, who was killed in Spain in 1330 while carrying the heart of his good friend and comrade King Robert I "the Bruce" to the Holy Land. Although Robert the Bruce was the hereditary enemy of Sir Fergus's father's family, once they swore allegiance they were always loyal to and were supported by both King David II (Robert the Bruce's son) and his wife Joanna (daughter of England's King Edward II).

The consequences of the Macdowall reversion of western Galloway to King David II of Scotland included the resignation of the kingship of Scotland by Edward Baliol in January 1356 to King Edward III of England. Edward then invaded Scotland in the east up to Edinburgh, destroying the lands and forfeiting their owners, including Makerstoun. The Douglases ambushed King Edward III on his way home on the outskirts of Melrose, near Makerstoun, and almost captured him.

In March of the same year, Sir William, Lord of Douglas, arranged a truce in Roxburgh. In June he had safe conduct to visit the captive King David II, to start arrangements for his release. From Maxwell's *History of Douglas*:

> But as a precaution against that rust which good chevaliers did
> so greatly dread should gather upon their arms in time of
> truce, he sought service under the King of France against the
> Black Prince, in time to share with the French chivalry the
> awful disaster of Poitiers (19th September 1356).

Sir William escaped, and seized Hermitage Castle from the English. But his uncle Sir Archibald the Grim, who had been knighted before the battle at 31 years of age by King John of France, fought it out, was captured, and later escaped by a ruse.

Fergus Macdowyll may have been there, but there is no record of it. It is more likely that Fergus allied himself with Sir William after he arranged the liberation of King David II from his English captivity in 1357 and was created the first Earl of Douglas in 1358. In any case, Sir William nominated Fergus to be Sheriff or Constable of Kirkcudbright castle with "ane three merk land" by royal charter from King David II in 1361. This gave Sir Fergus jurisdiction within the castle of Kirkcudbright and its precincts.

Sir Archibald Douglas was appointed Constable of Edinburgh Castle, Sheriff of Edinburgh, and Warden of the Western Marches. Then in 1369 King David II granted to Sir Archibald the lordship of the part of Galloway that lies between the Nith River at Dumfries and the Cree River at the present Newton Stewart—in other words, the whole shire or stewartry of Kirkcudbright. With that, Lord Archibald temporarily took up as his seat the Palace ("Burnt") Isle of Fergus Lord of Galloway and his heirs, on Loch Fergus above the town of Kirkcudbright.

Meanwhile, Fergus Macdowyll was still Constable within the old castle at the mouth of the Dee River (not the more modern castle in the town today), and the stage was set for Fergus to move ahead.

On February 22, 1371, King David II died and was succeeded by his nephew Lord Archibald's good friend, King Robert II, the Stewart. At the coronation, Archibald was dispatched to Paris on a special embassy "to swear on the King's soul the renewal of the ancient alliance between

Scotland and France." It is possible that Fergus Macdowyll was included in Archibald's entourage, for Fergus would have been classically schooled at home in French, Anglo-Saxon, Latin, and a little Greek, as well as being fluent in the Gaelic vernacular of the people of Galloway.

Wigtown (Western Galloway)

In about 1341, Sir Malcolm Fleming of Biggar conducted King David II and his wife Joanna from France to Scotland by ship. He was thereby elevated as the first Earl of Wigtown and was empowered to control the Macdowalls, MacCulachs, and other dispossessed native barons. Sir Malcolm's heir and grandson was Thomas Fleming, who also depended on the support of King David II.

Lord Archibald Douglas had the support of Robert II and the wealth from his new marriage to the Heiress of Bothwell, and he now proposed to subdue Wigtownshire. But Wigtown received him with hostility, because in 1332 he and Thomas Randolph, Earl of Moray, had wasted and plundered the district in revenge for their defeat near Perth by King Edward Baliol and the Macdowyll Gallowegians. Since the attempt to subdue Wigtown failed, Lord Archibald determined to buy it instead.

On October 7, 1372, Robert II confirmed the resignation and sale of the earldom of Wigtown by Thomas Fleming to Lord Archibald for 300 pounds.

> This dissipated Earl Thomas sold in consideration of a large
> sum of money, having been induced to sell his earldom on
> account of grievous feuds that had arisen between him and the
> more powerful of the ancient indigenous inhabitants of the
> earldom. (M'Kerlie)

Sir Fergus Macdowyll was knighted by Robert II in 1373 and rode into Wigtownshire with Lord Archibald. This facilitated the transition to the new Lordship under the Douglas banner from the traditional Lordship of ancient Galloway under the arms of the next male heirs, Fergus's older stepbrothers, Sir Dougall and John, who still held office in Wigtownshire. Sir Andrew Agnew wrote:

> This Sir Fergus attached himself to Douglas, a new phase in
> Galloway combinations; and hence Archibald the Grim was
> able, with less opposition, to advance to the Rhinns.

Said George Crawford:

> All vassals of the crown were forced to give up the charters
> and evidences of their estates and tenements, and if any of
> them were backward in it their houses were utterly destroyed
> and therein all the charters by which they held their
> possessions were irreversibly lost.

The Bruces had already done this to the Macdowyls of Garochloyne.

The "Black Douglas" (Archibald) demanded that the King's Sheriff of Western Galloway resign his lands and offices into his hands to be received back and held of him, together with "blackmail" payments for protection, with imprisonment and death in default. The Agnews refused, and after a siege of their castle on the islet of Lochnaw, they were allowed to return to their lands of Larne in Ireland (they later joined the Scots Court at Perth). Lochnaw Castle was, however, demolished with all in it and never restored on the loch. There is no record of what transpired at Garthland Castle at that time, but it was left intact and Sir Fergus's attention was given to his landed legacy outside Galloway.

Border Wars

The 1373 rolls of King Robert II include a charter recorded as having been granted to Fergus MacDougall/MacDowall of the Barony of Macarstoun, Yetham, & c., (in Roxburghshire) on the resignation of Margaret Fraser, his mother.[*] She could have given him his inheritance at this time to support his marriage and family. It is reasonable that Sir Fergus may have married the heiress of Garthland Castle, perhaps a Garth, but preferred not to be designated as "MacDougall/Macdowyll of Garthland."

Sir Fergus probably served with William, first Earl of Douglas (now also Earl of Mar) and with Archibald Lord of Galloway in certain border hostilities. In 1377 the dispossessed Scots Earl of March wasted his rightful heritage of Annandale and burned Roxburgh town, and in reprisal the English Earl of Northumberland crossed the border in strength and for three days ravaged Tweedale, including Makerstoun. The Douglases slipped around the superior forces of Northumberland and made a dash for Melrose, which the English Sir Thomas Musgrave was holding with a detachment.

> He timed his march so as to reach Melrose at midnight. It was the month of August, but they were overtaken by such a tempest of wind and rain that the pages dropped their master's spears for very cold, and the party had to take shelter in the woods. (Maxwell)

> They were full seven hundred lances, and two thousand others, whom I call lusty varlets, armed with hunting spears, dirks, and pointed staves. (Froissart)

> In the morning they sent out foragers, who encountered an English foraging party, whereby Musgrave received warning

---

[*] M'Kerlie, Vol. II, p. 466.

of the presence of the enemy. He turned out his force at once, and rode to give battle. When the two forces were in view of each other the Earl of Douglas bestowed knighthood upon his son (James afterwards 2nd Earl), and Sir Musgrave upon his. Thus ceremoniously were combats undertaken before chivalry began to wane. Then they set to with a will. (Maxwell)

Sir Archibald Douglas was a good knight, and much feared by his enemies; when near to the English he dismounted, and wielded before him an immense sword whose blade was two ells long (7 ½ ft.) which another could not have lifted from the ground; but he found no difficulty in handling it, and gave such terrible strokes that all on whom they fell were struck to the ground. (Froissart)

The English were routed; Musgrave and many of his followers were taken prisoners.

In the spring of 1380, the Douglases with 20,000 men invaded Cumberland and Westmoreland and returned with a large number of cattle, but they were followed by a smaller counter-raid across the Solway, bringing the English plague that became very destructive in Scotland. King Richard of England sent John of Gaunt, Duke of Lancaster, "with sufficient troops to wreak vengeance upon the Scots" (Maxwell) but all of these incursions were in violation of the old truce, which was now extended.

By way of assuring his legal succession in these hazardous times, Sir Fergus obtained a grant of confirmation of the Barony of Makerstoun by King Robert II to Fergus's elder son and heir, Sir Dungal Macdowel, on June 24, 1382.

Before the truce was over, Sir Fergus and the Earls of Douglas and Mar and March, and Lord Archibald overran and redeemed the counties of Annandale, Roxburgh, and Berwick from the English. They took the Bruces' ancient castle of Lochmaben in Dumfriesshire on February 4, 1384, expelled the English keeper, and dismantled the castle. On March 3, Sir Fergus had King Robert II confirm to his younger son Ughtred Macdowel an annual rent of 20 merks from his father out of Makerstoun, so clearly the younger generation was defending that seat when the Duke of Lancaster invaded Scotland up to Edinburgh and then withdrew. William Earl of Douglas then expelled the English from Teviotdale but died upon his return in May. He was buried at Melrose and was succeeded by his son James as the second Earl of Douglas, who was later killed at the famous battle of Otterburn.

Archibald the Grim became the third Earl of Douglas as well as Lord of Galloway, and was the most powerful subject in the realm. He and the Earl of Fife marched together into England and challenged King Richard

II's new Warden of the March, the Earl Marshal. He declined battle, which allowed the Scots to pillage and return home with booty.

In August 1400, King Henry IV invaded Scotland, and on Christmas Eve Archibald the Grim died at age 75 at Threave Castle. He was succeeded by his eldest legitimate son, Archibald, 28 years old and the "high-spirited" husband of Margaret, eldest daughter of King Robert III. The young Archibald was also a comrade in arms of Sir Fergus of Makerstoun, who would have been over 60 at the time.

At the same time, Sir Fergus's grandson, Sir Archibald Macdowell, was "of Makerstoun" as confirmed to him with the lands of Yetholme and Elystone (or Clifton) by King Robert III.

> In 1398 Sir Archibald M'Dowall grants a bond for the sum of foure skore and ten pound of gude mone, and lele of Scotlande in silver or in golde, because of his reliefe of his place of Malkerstoun, to be paid within two years in case as God forbede—Comoun were the raisings of baneris be betwixt the Kingrikis of Scotlande and Inglande. (M'Kerlie)

In September 1402, the new Douglas chief marched into England with Sir Fergus and 10,000 men to avenge an attack by George Dunbar, son of the Earl of March. They laid waste to all before them as far as Newcastle, collecting ample spoils. The followers included:

> The Earls of Murray and Angus, Sir Fergus Macdowall with his fierce and half-armed Galwegians, the heads of the noble houses of Erskine, Grahame, Montgomery, Seaton, Sinclair, Lesley, the Stewarts of Angus, Lorn and Durisdeer, and many other knights and esquires, embracing the greater part of the chivalry of Scotland—confident in their strength. (Mackenzie from Tytler)

> When the Scots had reached the village of Homildon, they beheld with surprise an English force ready to intercept them on their march, and took their ground on an eminence in the vicinity. The English were filled with unbounded rage at the sight of their plunderers; and the Earl of March could scarcely prevent the fiery Hotspur from leading his men to attack with their spears the Scots upon the heights. The English, however, were prevailed upon only to use their long bows, and thus from a distance gall their enemies who had closely formed on the hill. The effect these archers produced was terrible and destructive. Many of the bravest Scots being mortally wounded, fell down on the spot where they stood without having had an opportunity of once using their weapons. The horses, maddened by the showers of arrows, plunged and reared; whilst the dense mass of spearmen and "half naked Galwegians" presented the appearance of a hedgehog, bristled

over with a thousand shafts whose feathers were red with blood. But the Scots felt unwilling to lose the advantage of their situation by descending into the plain.

At length Sir John Swinton and Adam Gordon of Gordon with a hundred followers rushed down the declivity and made terrible havoc among the enemy; but these brave men were at last all slain. After their fall, the Scottish army being totally discomfited fled: the slaughter was dreadful. Nearly fifteen hundred were drowned in a vain attempt to ford the Tweed. (Balfour, Mackenzie)

The Earl himself and Sir Fergus Macdowyl of Garthland were wounded and made prisoners. Both were, however, released on paying ransom.

This information recorded by Sir James Balfour (the antiquary and Lord Lyon King of Arms under King Charles VI and I) in about 1635 implies that Sir Fergus was the first Macdowyll to come into possession of Garthland. It accounts for the genealogical confusion in our history of this time. The circumstance suggests that Sir Fergus did have the property and the Galloway support of his stepbrothers, troops and resources to wage war, provide hostages, and pay ransom for his release from captivity. To be spared from the slaughter, he must have had an outstanding suit of armor as did The Douglas.

Sir Fergus was with Douglas in 1412 when he went to France with a large company of knights and squires and entered into a bond of alliance with the Duke of Burgundy. Through his proximity to Douglas, Sir Fergus was a witness to many Douglas charters, including the disposition of Garthland in 1413–1414. At that time, the King of Scotland, James I, was captive in England and the Duke of Albany was Regent. King Henry IV (Bolingbroke) of England died that year—1413—and was succeeded by his son, Henry V of Agincourt fame.

Sir Fergus and his stepbrothers managed to recover the heritage lands of Gairachloyne and Lougan-Ellerig (Logan-Eldrig) together with his newly added Lochans where Garthland Tower stood. He obtained a charter granting them to him from the 4th Earl of Douglas, Lord of Galloway in 1413. Fergus then resigned all of them back into the Earl's hands to bestow them by charter (1414) on his nephew, Thomas Macdowyl, the surviving heritable head of the family (clan) in Galloway. We have no record of the wife of Sir Fergus, but she may have been the heiress of Garthland. Yet their sons held the fort of Makerstoun on the Borders for more than 30 years before those charters. Their sons were Dungal (Dougal/Duncan) and Ughtred (Uchtred), and the next heir was Archibald.

Makerstoun Kinsmen

Because Makerstoun and its neighbors were comparatively rich and much of the rest of North Britain so poor, the region was the target of raids and warfare over much of its history. Roxburghshire was an easy target, just across the border from England, and the estates were often invaded. But the mountains north and west of the Lowlands served to halt most invasions from proceeding farther. Thus, the Borders caught the brunt of much of the warfare and was occasionally occupied by the English.

Makerstoun had returned to Scottish governance just before Sir Fergus acquired the estate. He had his hands full with restoration of the property, and he and his successors turned to some of their MacDowall/McDougall kinsmen for help. Many apparently moved from Galloway and settled on or near the estate.

The vast majority of the newcomers presumably worked in farm-related jobs, ranging from herdsmen to carpenters. Few Scots anywhere could rise to middle class occupations such as lawyers and merchants because that sort of employment was rare and towns were few and far between.

The farmers, mostly in tenant houses scattered around the estate, helped the laird to tend the herds and to raise crops such as barley, oats, wheat, and rye. Dozens of the farmers settled into the community for the long haul.

The **Rev. Valerie Watson**, former minister of the Makerstoun Parish Church, whose family includes MacDougall ancestry, says that such migration at the time was not unusual even among the ordinary population, who were "far more mobile" than might be expected.

The graves of MacDougalls, McDougalls, MakDougalls, and other kinsmen in various spellings are numerous in cemeteries in and around Makerstoun, with tombstones dating back many centuries. The riverside cemetery at the ruins of the old Church of Scotland in nearby Ancrum, for example, contains many McDougall graves—some so old that the names and dates are almost undecipherable.

Sarah M. Cushman

Ancrum Gravestone

Sarah M. Cushman

**Ancient Ancrum church ruin,
where many McDougalls are buried**

One kinsman, the **Rev. Thomas MacDougal**, rose to serve the Makerstoun Parish as minister beginning in 1760. He took over after a series of problems in the church, reflecting the turmoil of the times. Reverend MacDougal's immediate predecessor, the Rev. William Walker, was suspended for several years, possibly because of activities connected with attempts to restore the Stewarts to the throne of Scotland.

Another predecessor, the Rev. William Turnbull, invited churchmen to attend the judging and burning of "witches in his parish on Wednesday and Thursday." The "detection of witches" was a matter of deep concern at the time to some clergymen in Scotland as well as America (as, for example, in Salem, Massachusetts).

In 1825, Anna-Maria Makdougal-Hay became heir to the Makerstoun estate. She married **Gen. Sir Thomas Brisbane**, who added the name Makdougal to his own family name.

His military career began in 1790 in Ireland. He was transferred to the Continent in 1792 and took part in action at Dunquerque, Newport, Nimeugen, and Tournay, where he was wounded. Beginning in 1796, he served in British campaigns in the West Indies, with action at St. Lucia, Trinidad, and Puerto Rico.

During the Napoleonic wars, he served in British Forces in Spain and France, where he was again wounded. He was awarded the thanks of the British Parliament at that time for his gallant conduct on the field.

In 1813, he was promoted to major general, and sent to North America the following year. There he led part of the British forces in action against the United States in Canada and New York.

When Napoleon returned to the leadership of France in 1815, Makdougal-Brisbane joined the British forces in Paris, commanding 12 brigades with 10,000 soldiers. When the Duke of Wellington reviewed those brigades, he exclaimed: "Had I had these regiments at Waterloo, I should not have wanted the Prussians." [*] Brisbane remained in France during British occupation after Napoleon's departure, and for his services was appointed Corresponding Member of the Institute of France.

In 1821, he was posted to Australia as Governor of New South Wales. The city of Brisbane is named for him. In 1825, he was promoted to lieutenant general and returned to Scotland, where he built an astronomical observatory at Makerstoun.

He was honored for his service to science with the presidency of the Royal Society of Edinburgh, and was created a baronet of Great Britain.

The most famous Makerstoun descendant was **Sir Walter Scott**, the author. As an invalid boy, he was inspired by frequent outings to the Pringles' Smailholm Tower four miles from Makerstoun. His novels combining elements of Scottish history, romance, and psychology (even before that science was widely known) helped to set the standards for fiction in the 19th century.

Walter was the great-great-grandson of Anne Isobel Makdougal of Makerstoun and Walter Scott. An unusual pair, the couple converted to the new Quaker faith, which was regarded with alarm by some people in the conservative Scottish establishment. Relatives took their children, William, Walter, and Isobel, to Makerstoun.

According to legend, Anne Isobel followed the children to Makerstoun, but the Makdougals did not allow her to enter. She is said to have fallen to her knees at the gate of her old home and prayed that the Makdougals and Scotts responsible would have no male heirs to carry on their line.

On June 20, 1665, Anne Isobel and Walter were ordered by the Scottish Privy Council to surrender the children, and Walter was jailed. Anne Isobel's curse seems to have worked—the direct male lines of both Makdougal and Scott families eventually died out in 1722.

---

[*] The Prussians were allies of the British in the battle at Waterloo.

Not all their relatives disapproved of the couple. Anne Isobel's brother William wrote a letter of apology to his brother-in-law, saying he was "sorry that our brothers should continue in ther wonted malise and un-Christian dealings with you." William signed off with "deer luv to my sister yourself and Christian, I am your brother till death, Will Macdougal." The affair rankled the Makdougals and Scotts for generations.

Anne Isobel's second son, Walter, who was Sir Walter Scott's great-grandfather, turned out to be as opinionated as his parents. He was known as "Beardie" because in his adulthood he took a vow to avoid shaving his beard until and if the Stewarts were restored to rule. Much later, Sir Walter expressed his admiration for his great-grandfather in the epic poem, "Marmion":

> The simple sire could only boast
> That he was loyal to his cost.
> The banished race of kings revered
> And lost his land—but kept his beard.

Sir Walter noted that it

> would have been well that his zeal had stopped there. But he
> took arms and intrigued in their [the Stewarts'] cause, until he
> lost all he had in the world, and, as I have heard, ran a narrow
> risk of being hanged, had it not been for the interference of
> Anne, Duchess of Buccleuch and Monmouth, the head of his
> family, widow of the Duke of Monmouth of unfortunate
> memory. Afterwards, he was forced to live in strict retirement,
> subsisting mainly on the fortune of his wife.

Sir Walter Scott was born in Edinburgh in 1771. His father was a lawyer, and persuaded young Walter to enter that profession. His heart, however, lay with writing, and he began to compose poetry.

It was his novels that led to worldwide fame. His first novel, *Waverley*, was about the failed attempt to reinstall the Stewarts as kings. Other books, including *Rob Roy*, *Ivanhoe*, *The Pirate*, and *Redgauntlet*, followed, and he found himself one of the most popular authors of his time.

In 1818, Scott became a Baronet, and he was a co-host to King George IV on a visit to Scotland that helped to reestablish the popularity of Scottish culture. Later his reputation waned, but Scott remains one of the most successful novelists of the past two centuries. Always proud of his heritage, he treasured the memories of stories told to him about his ancestors, and the coat of arms of his Makdougal lineage is prominently displayed in his study at the Abbotsford estate on the Tweed River, close to Makerstoun. He died in 1832.

❋ ❋ ❋

Over the years, the population of Makerstoun has varied considerably. Before the end of the 18th century, the parish had about 1,000 inhabitants. In 1981, there were 132. Change in land management resulted from a population explosion just when landlords were trying to make their holdings more efficient by clearing out small farmers. The result was that hundreds of Scots marched southward into England where jobs were more plentiful, and others boarded ships for parts of the world where cheap land was available.

Typical of the times, one Makerstoun area family—**James McDougall**, born in Kelso, and his wife Agnes, from nearby Ancrum— emigrated to America with their four children in 1796. Near Argyle, New York, they bought a small farm and joined a McDougall colony that totaled 14 men and women plus children. By the early 1900s, descendants of the colony totaled more than 3,000, spread across the United States and elsewhere. The number is estimated to have doubled since then.

Another family making a similar move from the Borders was that of **William McDougal**, whose son William was born in 1782. The younger William was baptized in Ednam Church, about five miles from Makerstoun, and married Janet Sword in 1806. They lived in Dalkeith and Edinburgh, and had three sons. In 1819, they emigrated to America, first to Pennsylvania and then to Beallsville, Ohio. The middle son, Thomas, stayed in Ohio, while the others moved to other states. Today, almost all "McDougals" in eastern Ohio trace their lineage to William McDougal of Ednam.

According to records possessed by family historian **Gregory J. McDougall** of New South Wales, Australia, some of the earliest European settlers of Australia included his ancestors, the McDougalls of Makerstoun.

Makerstoun Today

At Makerstoun, surprisingly little appears outwardly to have changed in the past two centuries. Makerstoun House, rebuilt in 1973 after a fire, stands again as the most prominent feature on the estate. The Tweed River still flows quietly, and is now a favored location for paid expeditions to fish for salmon. The rolling valleys and hills abound, as before, in livestock and crops.

Lady Mary Biddulph, whose Maitland family bought Makerstoun in 1921, lived in and restored Makerstoun House from 1961 to 1997, and studied "the history of the name and the estate." Her son, the fifth Baron Biddulph, lives there now.

MAKERSTOUN HOUSE

Courtesy of The Rt. Hon. Mary Lady Biddulph

**As restored in 1974 to William Adam's plans of 1714–21 as drawn up by
Henry Macdougal and built by Henry Hay Macdougal in 1790**

❀ ❀ ❀

Cadets

Macdowall/Makdougal of Makerstoun is the earliest confirmed baronial cadet (branch) of Macdowall of Garthland, and the pro tem. senior cadet of MacDougall/Macdowyl of Gairachloyne, and thereby of the Lowland MacDougalls. The branch's motto is "Fear God."

In the parish of Makerstoun, the Makdougals gave rise to or supported other armigerous branches. Nearby Stodrig may have had more recent origin from Garthland, but MacDougall/Macdowell of Lodvica in Sweden, the name Duwall in Estonia, and that of von Wahl in Latvia and Germany, all baronial in their own right, are descended from Makerstoun.

Macdowell/M'dowall of Stodrig

René A. van Iterson, Fergus D. H. Macdowall,
and W. Lesley McDowall

According to Nesbit, "the first of this family was Thomas M'Dowall, designated burgess of Edinburgh, who bought the lands of Stodrig, in the shire of Roxburgh, from John of Meryden, as by charter granted to the said Thomas, the 10th of July 1520, which I have seen. From him is lineally descended the present Thomas M'Dowall of Stodrig."

No descent from Macdowall of Makerstoun has been recorded.

Nesbit describes the arms as "Azure, a lion rampant argent, gorged with an open crown or" (for old Macdowall/McDouall); "and between his fore paws a heart proper" (for Douglas); "crest a lion's paw" (for old Garthland); "motto Vincere vel Mori" (as for Garthland) "which arms were cut upon a stone above a door of the house of Stodrig in Teviotdale in the year 1593, as the stone bears."

These arms were mounted on Stodrig House by Thomas MakDougall, 3rd of Stodrig, in 1593, and show that he was descended from Garthland and not through Makerstoun because the Fraser cinquefoils—ornamental design—were excluded. He also reverted to the Garochloyne spelling of MacDougall, as did William Macdougal, 11th of Makerstoun, at the same time, 1613.

New arms had been rematriculated before Nisbet illustrated them in 1816 with demi-lion crest (as for Logan) and motto *Cor aut Nihil*. These also indicate M'Douall-Douglas connections.

A lineal descendant who rose to prominence was Professor William Macdowell of Stodrig ("Gvilielmvs Makdowel" in Latin) at Groningen, northeast Holland. He was born in October 1590, in the parish of Makerstoun, the son of Thomas Macdowell of Stodrig and Johanna Ker. Thomas's mother was Beatrix, daughter of William Douglas, hereditary Sheriff, and Johanna was daughter of Andrew Car of Greynhead.

William was educated at Musselburgh Grammar School (1595–1603), Carlson Grammar School (1604) and St. Leonard's College of the University of St. Andrews, where he was awarded the Ph. M. degree (1605–1609). His career started as a founding professor of divinity and philosophy at the University of Groningen, the Netherlands, where he also achieved the L.L.D. degree.

Archives of Fergus D. H. Macdowall

William Macdowell of Stodrig, a founding professor of divinity and philosophy at the University of Groningen, the Netherlands

In 1617 he married Lady Bernadina van Fritema, daughter of Johan Clant, Lord Mayor of Groningen. They had two daughters, including Johanna Emilia who later married Ulrich van Ewsum. In 1640 in the Aa-kerk of Groningen, Professor Makdowel married Elisabeth Alberda, lady of Luusemaborg in Feerwerd, widow of Lord Syds van Botnia. Their home was "Elmersma" near Hoogkerk. His nephew conveyed some Stodrig land to him in 1644.

Archives of Fergus D. H. Macdowall

**L-shaped house "Elmersma" of Lady Elisabeth
and Prof. William Makdowel at Hoogkerk**

As a nobleman of Hoogkerk, close to Groningen, "Gullielmus Makdowell" was associated with the War Council of the City and County of Groningen (1627–1650). He was a vociferous, loyal supporter of the British crown against the parliaments of Oliver Cromwell. King Charles II was still in exile from 1649 to 1660 in France, Germany and Flanders, and in 1650, he appointed William as his ambassador to The Hague. William moved to "Newelant" ("new land") in the southern province of Zuid-Holland, where The Hague is the capital in the jurisdiction of the Estates of Holland. While there in 1653, William sent his signet ring with his arms engraved to his Scottish relation Lord Ker of Nisbet, the first Earl of Lothian, perhaps to petition a grant of arms.

These arms (on the shield) were: Per pale dexter, azure a lion rampant contourne (turned around as a difference from Galloway); argent with three cinquefoils argent in the field (for Fraser, canting to Makerstoun); and sinister, per fess, in the first a stag's head caboshed (cut off) (for Ker), and in the second quarter a heart (for Douglas). Above this on an open-visored helm with a mantling of his liveries issuant from a crest coronet or is set for a crest a demi-lion rampant contourne crowned or. The orientation of the helm shows knighthood (in the United Kingdom) and it is very likely that King Charles II knighted William, probably as "Sir William Makdowel of Newelant" to serve as his ambassador.

Upon the restoration of Charles II to the crown of the United Kingdom, the King galloped from Brussels, with which England was still at war under Spain, across the frontier to Breda to sign the declaration of unconditional restoration. At the end of April 1660, 18 deputies from the Dutch States-General went to Breda to invite Charles, with expenses, to come to The Hague, and Sir William would have been with them.

At The Hague, they were busy with two weeks of business and receptions until May 23, when the royal party and entourage took ship for Dover. There they were welcomed by General Monk, who had brought the Scots Army from Edinburgh to London for this purpose.

Sir William was based in London until he became ill in 1665 and resigned his ambassadorship. He died on March 21, 1666, and was interred beside his wife at "de grote kerk van Hoogkerk." His arms are displayed with those of Fritema on a large plaque in the aisle of the restored church. Coincidentally, the town archives of Groningen record the marriage of "Jonker (nobleman) Robbert Makdowell" and Anna Sophia ten Ham, in Ulenburgh on March 17, 1666. An Allan Macdowel married Jenneken Schutten at Deventer in 1707.

Professor William Makdowel's dwellings near Hoogkerk and in Groningen City are still identifiable and some are in excellent state. He is commemorated at the University of Groningen, and by the church and "The MacDowell Pipe Band" at Hoogkerk, where Pipe Major Benne P. de Jong composed the march tune, "Professor MacDowell."

Groningen newspaper, courtesy Rene van Iterson, July 1996

Presentation of Pipe Banner to MacDowell Pipe Band of Highkirk, ND, in 1996 (from left, Pipe Major Benne de Jong, historian & Hon. State Piper René van Iterson, and Fergus Macdowall of Garthland)

Pedigree of the Makdowalls/McDougalls of Stodrig

W. Lesley McDowall

As far as has been accepted, up to the present time, at the College of arms, the line commences with Thomas Makdowell of Stotharig.

1. THOMAS MAKDOWELL of Stotharig/Stodrig in the Parish of Makerstoun, Roxburghshire, who purchased from his kinsman Andrew M'Dowell of Makerstoun, lands called "Auldsyde" by charter dated 20th August 1508. From this time there is evidence of two distinct families—of Makerstoun and of Stodrig. Thomas was a witness to a deed in 1536 and was succeeded at Stodrig by his son Alexander.

2. ALEXANDER MAKDOWELL of Steidrig acquired various lands in the Barony of Makerstoun between 1553 and 1567. He died in December 1568, and by his last will and testament made by himself at his dwelling place of Steidrig on November 18, 1568, desired that his body might be buried in the aisle in McCairston (Makerstoun Church).

3. THOMAS MAKDOUGALL of Stodridge, son and heir of the above Alexander, was underage in 1568. He is mentioned in several charters and acted as trustee for James McDougall of Makerston in 1608. He was succeeded by his son Alexander.

4. ALEXANDER MAKDOUGALL of Stethridge (Stodrig) is mentioned in deeds circa 1618 and 1621, and married Helen Hangitsyde the widow of Alexander Weddell of Little Newton, Berwickshire. Alexander had a brother, Prof. William McDowell, who presided over the Council of War in the provinces of Freizland and Groningen in 1620, and he had a sister Elizabeth who married James Haig of Bemerside first and Robert Ker of Greneherd second. In 1619 Alexander Makdougall had a bond from his nephew Andrew Haig of Bemerside.

5. THOMAS MACDOUGALL of Stodrige succeeded his father Alexander and in 1644 ratified a disposition in favor of his uncle, Prof. William McDougall of Höogkerk, The Netherlands. In 1659 he was in possession of a rent from the lands of Bemerside, and had a bond confirming the same in 1661. His wife's name was Johan Vavasoir. His elder son Alexander McDougall married Anne, eldest daughter of Andrew Ker of Little Dean, but apparently died without issue.

6. THOMAS MACDOUGALL of Stodrig, younger son of the last named Thomas, married in 1676 Isobel, sister of Robert Merser of

Coldstream, Berwickshire. He had seisin (deed of possession) of a house and land there in this year and obtained the lands of "Auldsyde," Stodrig, and Netherlongton in Makerstoun Parish as heir to his great-grandfather Thomas (who was the grandson of the original grantee of 1508) in 1687, but continued to reside at Coldstream until 1699. His wife Isobel Merser died on or about October 2, 1698, and he remarried a certain Isobel Broun, widow of Robert Geddes of Cornhill, County Northumberland, who was party to a bond with her stepson Alexander MacDougall in 1708.

7.   THOMAS MACDOUGALL of Stodrig was the elder son of the above Thomas MacDougall. He was served heir to his grandfather in 1701 and appears to have disposed of the lands in Makerstoun Parish between 1714 and 1732.

8.   ALEXANDER MCDOUGALL was the younger son of Thomas by Isobel Merser, served as a Dragoon under Captain Douglas in 1701, and was of the Earl of Hyndford's regiment in 1704. He was married at Coldstream in 1700 to Margaret, second daughter and apparently co-heir of the Rev. William Whillas, sometime Minister of Lessingham, County Norfolk. He was living in Edinburgh from 1721 to 1724 when he made some claim upon the estate of Sempill of Cathcart.

9.   ALEXANDER MCDOUGALL, elder son of the above Alexander and Margaret was baptized at Coldstream in 1713. He married Janet Atchison, by whom he had a son Alexander. He obtained land in Birgham in the parish of Eccles, Berwickshire, in 1765 and was living there in 1767.

10. ALEXANDER MCDOUGALL, son of the above Alexander, was baptized at Ladykirk in 1750 and married Isobel Foster at Coldstream in 1778. He was buried at Birgham in 1788. This is the man, according to his grandson's statement, who was taken by a press gang and served in the war with the Spaniards on the coasts of South America.

11. JAMES MCDOUGALL, elder son of the above Alexander, was born at Coldstream in 1779. He married Alison, daughter of John Watson of Maxwelltown, and had, with other issue, a son Alexander.

12. ALEXANDER MCDOUGALL of Manchester was "The Founder of The Firm" and founder of a prolific family as in Ref: A.R. 1.219 at the College of Arms, London, and in their own publication, *The McDougall Brothers and Sisters*, Blackheath Press, 1923, which should make them traceable to the present time.

MacDougall/Macdowall of Lodvica, Duwall, and von Wahl

Fergus D. H. Macdowall, Kenth Berg, and Henning von Wahl

Lodvica

In his discussion of arms, Nisbet gives a description of "M'Dougall Barons of Lodvica" who descended from the family of Makerstoun. The descent is clarified and extended in Elgenstierna's publication "Svenska adelus äattartavlor."

Thomas Macdowell (Tomas MacDougall), who died in 1618, was the second son of Thomas Macdowell, eighth of Makerstoun, and his wife, Janet Scott, heiress of Howfaslet (which also led to Lord Napier and Scotts of Thirlestane). In 1571 the Thomas Macdowells were succeeded by Patrick Macdowell (Patrik MacDougall), who married Margaret Nisbet, a daughter of the chief of that name anciently in the lands of Nisbet. His son "Robert" (actually Albert or Albrekt) (1541–1641) initially married Mary Anderson (Maria Anderseen) and was succeeded by Colonel James M'Dowell, who in turn married Anna, daughter of George Vanderberg, of Saggadt in Eastland (then in Sweden, now in Estonia).

According to Nisbet, their heir became "Colonel Gustavus M'Dowell Baron of Lodvica." Apparently in preparation to petition heraldic arms:

> He, to show his noble descent from Scotland, obtains a birth-
> brieve, or certificate, of his paternal and maternal descents,
> upon the declarations of several persons of good quality,
> before the magistrates of Edinburgh, 2nd March 1656, which
> stands there recorded as cited above. The "persons" were "the
> most considerable barons and gentlemen of Teviotdale and the
> Merse." (Nisbet, Vol. I, p. 285)

Finally in 1674, Gustavus received his patent of nobility when King Charles XI of Sweden granted him his coat of arms: quarterly first azure, a lion argent, crowned or (for Macdowall); second gules, an arm in armour argent, holding a cross-crosslet fitchee azure (for MacDougall); third, or a lymphad sable (for MacDougall); fourth or a rock sable in base (for Macdowall), and in chief, two salmons naiant in fesse, proper. Above the arms is a dove on a baronial crown (probably for Lodvica) and above two helms are crest-coronets (probably for Macdowell or MacDougall); over all is the Makerstoun motto "Fear God." Baron Colonel Gustavus clearly adopted the Highland elements of arms to emphasize his ancient patronym of MacDougall, albeit from Galloway in the Lowlands.

The son and heir of Gustavus was Colonel Alexander M'Dowell Baron of Lodvica, and it seems that he was succeeded by his step-cousin, a Duwall.

Duwall

Col. Alexander M'Dowell of Lodvica's great-grandfather, "Albrekt MackDuwall" from Makerstoun, was 53 years old when he started a new family in 1594. He moved to Sweden and married his second wife Elsa, daughter of Hans von Bredau of Kremmen (Kremnand) and his wife, Elizabet von Plessen. Albrekt and Elsa had two sons, Jakob Mac-Dougall, friherre (baron) Duwall (1589–1634) and Mauritz MacDougall, naturalized to Duwall (1603–1655). Albrekt died in his 100th year in 1641.

The heraldic arms of Duwall were registered in 1632, and show modified devices of Highland MacDougall and Argyle, but with a bird for the crest. Other sons Axel and Tobias MackDougall, also claiming to be "of Mackerston," together with Mauritz produced prolific branches of Duwalls. General Jakob is written as "arfherre" of Mackerston and "friherre" (baron) of Lodvica, and he had two eminent sons. Lodvica does not appear subsequently.

Alexander Nisbet, A System of Heraldry, p. 409
Duwall Heraldic Arms

The Mac-Dougalls of Duwall produced more than 60 sons, most of whom maintained the noble Swedish military reputation in the family. However, many of the direct lines ended with daughters. The last male heir was Adalbert Fridolf Magnus Mac-Dougall of Duwall, who died March 5, 1923. He was followed by his cousin, the Baroness Sigrid Ulrika Charlotta Mac-Dougall of Duwall, who married Count Adolf Gabriel Barnekov. She died September 13, 1926, but she had perpetuated her patronym in her eldest son, Count Kjell Ragnar Mac-Dougall Barnekow. He died in 1958, and his son, Count Kjell Edward Alveric Mac-Dougall Barnekow, died in 1965. This left his son Henrik (born 1944) and his grandsons Fredrik (born 1978) and Carl-Henrik (born 1980) to carry the name Mac-Dougall Barnekow into the future.

Von Wahl

Robert (Albert, Albrecht) Macdowell (MacDougall, MagDuwalt, MackDuwall) started another family with his third wife, Ursula von Stralendorff, from another noble German family of Mecklenburg, in 1651. For this family, the surname was contracted further to de/du/von Wall/Wahl. A son, Axel de/von Wall/Wahl was recently accepted as actually the above-mentioned Axel Duwall. His descendant, Johann Heinrich (von) Wahl (1725–1795), was the last in Latvia when his son, Carl Gustav von Wahl, and six grandsons established their own estates in Germany through the 19th century. Their heirs are widely distributed today under their unique family arms, and they may be the last traceable, living direct line from the barony of Makerstoun in Scotland.

Alexander Nisbet, A System of Heraldry, p. 27
Arms of the Family v. Wahl

MacDowall/Duwall/de Wall/von Wahl Family in Sweden and Baltic Provinces of Estonia and Livonia

Henning von Wahl

Our German-Baltic family "von Wahl" only recently discovered through my genealogical research at the Krigsarkivet (Military Archives) and Rigsarkivet (National Archives) in Stockholm that we are a branch of the Scottish-Swedish family, "Duwall."

Robert Albrecht

In 1594, the Scotsman Robert Albrecht MacDowall/Dougall entered the royal Swedish armed forces. Born in Makerston (also spelled Makerstoun) on the Borders of Scotland in 1541, he belonged to the old Scottish noble family MacDowall/Dougall of Makerston.

A younger son, he decided to take up a career as an officer in the Scottish army, in which he served as captain. But, like many Scots, he emigrated to the Continent to escape the frequent Anglo-Scottish wars and to find a better life. He entered into military service in north Germany, probably for the Elector of Brandenburg and for the Duke of Mecklenburg/Germany.

There he married three wives in succession who were members of the north German nobility. The first was Maria Andersen. The second was Elsa von Bredow, daughter of Hans von Bredow of Mecklenburg and Elisabeth von Plessen. Both were of well-known noble families still existing today. Elsa had four sons: Albrecht, Christian, Jacob, and Hans.

Elsa died after the birth of her fourth son, Hans. So Albrecht MacDowall married Ursula von Stralendorf, also from Mecklenburg, daughter of Joachim von Stralendorf and Elisabeth von Wackerbarth. The noble family of Stralendorf also is flourishing today. Their five sons —Axel, Joachim, Mauritz, Johann, and Tobias—and three daughters were all born after 1594 in Sweden. They probably grew up speaking German within the family because Albrecht had lived for decades in Germany and his wife was German.

In 1610, Albrecht became administrator of the royal Swedish castles of Örbyhus and Tierp. All of his nine sons chose military careers, and, except for Mauritz and Tobias, all died in the Thirty Years War (1618–1648) in Germany.

Jacob and Axel

Jacob, born of the second marriage, became a famous Swedish general and led a Swedish army to Silesia, then part of the Hapsburg empire. He died in 1634, and was posthumously created a Swedish "freiherre" (baron), thus founding the baronial family Duwall in Sweden.

Courtesy of Henning v. Wahl
Gen. Jacob MackDuwall and his wife Anna von Berg

Jacob's brother, Mauritz, born in 1603, who became a Swedish colonel, also was ennobled in 1638. So the family MacDowall became naturalized in Sweden as Duwall. But the old Scottish name, MacDowall or Dougall, also was still in use.

A son born of Albrecht's third marriage was the officer, Axel Duwall. In 1628, he took part in the successful defense of the city of Stralsund against the siege of Field Marshal Wallenstein.

Two years later, after the landing of a Swedish army on the island of Usedom on the Baltic Sea, Axel fell as a colonel of the Swedish infantry during the siege of Wolgast. Axel was buried in the beautiful church of St. Nikolai in Stralsund. The King, Gustaf-Adolf, who knew Axel well, was present. An epitaph for Axel with a German inscription was unfortunately lost at the end of World War II. But a panel with a German inscription recalling Axel's services for the Crown still exists and has been restored by order of our family.

Shortly before Axel fell, he married again. We do not know her name, but she is explicitly mentioned as his "wife" in a document by which Axel received the estate of Hallkved in Sweden, donated by King Gustaf-Adolf in recognition of Axel's extraordinary military services for the Swedish Crown.

Axel's widow accompanied her brother-in-law and his wife, Anna, with the Swedish army to Silesia, then a province of the Hapsburgs, emperors of the Holy Roman Empire. It was common then for soldiers' families to accompany the army in order to maintain their daily livelihood. Anna died in Silesia and Jacob died in 1634 in Breslau. They are remembered by a magnificent gravestone in the Nikolai Church at Stralsund.

Joachim Adolf

Axel's widow gave birth to a son, Joachim Adolf, in 1630/31 in Silesia. Joachim was the name of a younger brother of Axel, as well as the name of the father of Axel's mother. The name Adolf also showed Axel's close personal ties to King Gustaf-Adolf. In the Swedish documents, we found his surname also spelled as Duwalt or De Wall/Wahl. I suppose that Adolf chose to separate the name because the syllable "de" or "du," or "von" in German and "of" in English stands for a noble family.

Joachim Adolf grew up in Silesia. His mother did not return to Sweden with the Swedish army. She may have found after the withdrawal of the Swedish troops a new existence in peaceful Silesia, which had a strong Protestant minority.

Joachim Adolf followed the military tradition of the family and became an officer in the imperial Hapsburg army, but later transferred to the royal Swedish army. This may have happened during the Swedish-Polish war (1655–1660) when the Hapsburgs supported the Catholic House of Wasa, then kings of Poland, against the Protestant kings of Sweden. Joachim Adolf probably knew about his aunt Anna, Jacob's wife, who came from the old noble family, "von Berg," who belonged to the German nobility of the then Swedish provinces of Estonia and Livonia (the old Livonia now lies in both Estonia and Latvia). Joachim Adolf settled in Livonia as a "land owner of an estate" after 1682. I suppose he was an administrator or tenant of this estate.

The Swedish Crown, because of its many wars, was dangerously short of money and started to reduce the old feudal estates held by the nobility since the Middle Ages. Some of the properties were sold and the proceeds reverted to the Crown. Other lands were sold to the highest bidder. Joachim Adolf probably was an administrator for the Crown for such an expropriated estate. These estates provided the army with food, horses, armaments, and money.

But such procedures created strong opposition among the nobility, and some nobles were punished severely. One nobleman, Reinhold von Patkul, and some of his companions were executed by the Swedish Crown after they formed an anti-Swedish coalition of the traditional enemies of Sweden: Denmark, Russia, and Poland, as well as a new opponent, Prussia.

In the Great Nordic War (1700–1721), Sweden fought the coalition for domination of the Baltic Sea and its surrounding countries. Joachim Adolf de Wall/Wahl fought as an officer in the Swedish Dragoons Regiment von Meyerfeldt. But he was getting older, and he retired as a captain in 1705.

Johann Georg

One of his sons, Johann Georg (de) Wall, born in Stockholm in 1682, also became a soldier in the Swedish army. In 1702, he started like his father as a dragoon in the Livonian Dragoons Regiment of General von Schlippenbach. He took part in several battles against Russia and Czar Peter the Great and probably in the Battle of Poltawa (1709) which ended in a disastrous defeat for the Swedish army. As a result, Swedish King Charles XII fled to the Ottoman Empire (now Turkey).

The remainder of the Swedish army retired to the Swedish provinces of Estonia and Livonia which were soon conquered by the army of Czar Peter. Johann Georg escaped to then-Swedish Finland together with the defeated Swedish army.

Johann's next deployment was to the Swedish fortress of Wiborg in Finland which guarded the border with Russia. Czar Peter laid siege to Wiborg and conquered it in 1710.

Johann was a prisoner of war of Russia until 1722 when he was freed after the end of the Great Nordic War, which devastated parts of northern Europe. The former Swedish provinces of Estonia and Livonia lost two-thirds of their population as they came under Russian rule. At the same time, the reduction of the old feudal estates was canceled, and the German nobility retained its dominant position as landowners and administrators and in the area's Protestant religion.

After his long and hard experience as a Russian prisoner of war, Johann Georg did not want to stay in the ruined, now-Russian provinces. So he and his wife emigrated to Sweden in order to continue his profession as a soldier and provide an income for his family. However, as his military career had not been very successful and his old regiment had been dismissed, he ended as a staff sergeant in the Swedish artillery. We do not know why he did not become an officer during his service in the war against Russia, except that promotion had been hindered by his captivity.

Johann Georg and his wife from Livonia had several children, but most died in Sweden in the hard times after the Nordic War. Only one son, Johann-Heinrich, survived. Johann Georg died in about 1735. His widow, having no income, returned to Livonia where she had relatives.

Johann-Heinrich

Johann-Heinrich grew up in Livonia without a father. But his mother succeeded in providing an excellent education for her son. He had a successful career as an administrator of several big estates, and made a fortune as a tenant of estates. In 1795, he was ennobled as "von Wahl" by the Holy Roman Emperor with the argument that the family always had belonged to the old nobility.

Alexander Nisbet, A System of Heraldry. 31

Johann Heinrich v. Wahl

The imperial diploma, still in the possession of our family, explicitly and formally acknowledges Johann Heinrich's ancestors: his father, Johann Georg, his grandfather Joachim Adolf, and his great-grandfather Axel Wahl. The document mentions that the ancestors of Johann Heinrich were proved by "credible documents." Unfortunately, those documents were lost in a fire in 1801.

Our family were members of the Ritterschaften—assembly of the land-owning nobility—who represented and administered the provinces of Estonia, Livonia, and Kurland since the Middle Ages by their feudal parliament (Landtag). A seat in this parliament was connected to the property of an estate. Those parliaments and the feudal administration fulfilled until 1920 the whole inner self-government of those provinces, quite similar to the old feudal parliaments in Scotland and England.

One of Johann Heinrich's sons was Karl-Gustav von Wahl. He made a fortune as an administrator and tenant of several big estates when he supplied provisions for the Russian army against the invasion of Napoleon. He bought several big estates in Estonia and Livonia. That formed the economic basis of the wealth of our von Wahl family, which continued until 1919 when the newly-founded countries of Estonia and Latvia expropriated all the lands of the German landowners. The various houses of our family lost about 125,000 acres.

Modern Times

The last members of our family left the Baltic states in 1939/40 after the Hitler-Stalin Treaty, before Estonia and Latvia were occupied by the Soviet Union. Most von Wahls went to Germany; others to Finland, France, and Belgium. After World War II, nearly a quarter of our family emigrated to Canada.

Over 100 years ago, several von Wahls started genealogical research in order to find the origin of the Swedish officer, Axel Wahl. During the Thirty Years War and the Great Nordic War and in the fire of 1801, our family lost all documents about Axel, Joachim Adolf, and Johann Georg. We knew nothing about our ancestor, Axel Wahl.

Then in 1937, my father, Otto, found the first documents about Joachim Adolf De Wall/Wahl in the Swedish National Archives. I started further research in Sweden in 1998 and 2004. With the help of some well-known Swedish genealogists, we found proofs for the existence of Johann Georg (de) Wall and Axel de Wahl/Wall/Duwall. Now we have also found out the Scottish origin of Axel's family. His ancestors and our line of descent from Axel to Johann Heinrich is now acknowledged officially by the editorial commission of the "Handbook of the Nobility" (formerly the "Gotha") in 2008.

Henning von Wahl
Henning von Wahl, with wife Bettina and son Nikolai

Westward Exodus

Leo B. McDowell

The County Antrim McDowells left Scotland in 1584 for Ulster. So states an account found in early correspondence relating to the work of Mary Kyle McDowell, a Protestant nun and genealogist in the mid to late 1800s. Perhaps not so coincidentally, 1584 is also the year that Uchtred Macdowall, 10th of Garthland, had his summons deleted by the royal warrant (19 August 1584) for his part in the Ruthven Raid affair.

Although family chroniclers state that Uchtred sought sanctuary in France before his pardon, it is well documented that the phrase "exiled to France" during these times often simply meant "left the isle of Britain."

The Irvines are close kin to the McDowells and fellow Covenanters from Scotland, and are credited with building their home in Gleno, County Antrim, in 1585. Thus, the 600-year-old book described by L. Boyd in *The Irvines and Their Kin* may shed more light on when the McDowells actually arrived to settle in County Antrim.

> There is no district in all of Ireland so rich in armorial bearings as the neighborhood of Lame. The churchyards of Carncastle, Glynn, and Raloo abound with them. The churchyard of Raloo is over-grown with long grass and weeds, so as to be almost inaccessible. But one may pull aside obstructions and remove lichens from the tall gray tombstones; trace the arms carved upon them, and read the names of the Craigs, McDowells, Crawfords, Boyds, and others.

> There is an old book, more than six hundred years old (I was told), that I found at Fair Hill, near Larne. It had belonged to successive sextons for hundreds of years, from the dates it contained, the last one being 1775, and giving a description of the flag adopted by the American Colonies. It is written in longhand, and has pen-pictures of the Coats of Arms of the Carlisles, Earls of Kilmarnock, McDowells, Irvines, Johnstons, Crawfords, and Blairs, and many others not connected with this history. In the beginning of the book this appears, written in a clerklike hand: "Nobilitatis virtus non stemma"—"Virtue, not pedigree, is the mark of nobility."

Mary Semple of Mounthill, near Larne in County Antrim, Ulster (an Irish genealogist from the early 1900s), wrote about the McDowells and associated families in County Antrim. Mary Semple researched and presented extensive genealogies on the Blair, Irvine, Knox, and Lyle families as well—families which bear close ties of kinship to the McDowells in Ulster, Canada, and America.

The research of Mary Semple was done via family Bibles, personal interviews and stories passed down by word of mouth from living relatives, other written documentation, and through civil and church records. Mary Semple also had access to the records of the Presbyterian Church in Raloo near Larne, town and civil records, and the Raloo Presbyterian Church graveyard where many of the McDowells and related families are buried, including Margaret Irvine McDowell (died 1728)—the wife of Ephraim McDowell of Virginia.

Some of the oldest McDowell headstones in the Raloo churchyard bear the coats-of-arms and mottos of Macdowalls of Garthland. This supports Mary Semple's claim that the McDowells of Gleno, Raloo Parish, County Antrim, Ulster descend from that family.

According to Mary Semple,

> Uchtred [Macdowall, 8th of Garthland] succeeded his grandfather in 1513 and married his cousin Marion, daughter of Sir Alexander Stewart of [Gurlies]. Their son, John succeeded in 1531 and married Margaret, daughter and heiress of John Campbell. He was killed at Pinkie in 1547. His son, Uchtred, married Margaret, daughter of Sir Hugh Kennedy and their 'seventh' son, John McDowell came to Gleno, parish of Raloo near Larne, Ireland in (by?) 1595 as a political exile where he married Mary Wylie. Their [grand?]son Thomas married Ann Locke. Their son Ephriam married his cousin Margaret Irvine.

> The above Ephriam McDowell married Margaret Irvine who died, left Gleno with two of his sons, two daughters and three brothers-in-law for America. They sailed from Larne in a sailing ship called the 'George and Ann' on May 29, 1731. After a short stay in Pittsburgh, Pa., they settled in Virginia. He was a lad of 16 when he was pressed to the siege of Londonderry. He went with King William to the Battle of the Boyne and shod the King's white horse the night before the battle. He had been learning to be a blacksmith with his father. The house where he lived and the shop where he wrought are still to be seen in the lovely village of Gleno.

> All the (then present) McDowells of Raloo are descended from him through his eldest son Thomas who remained in Gleno. His brother-in-law Alexander Irvine was one of the 'Apprentice Boys' who closed the gates of Derry in the face of King James' Army.

> Ephriam was one (of the sons) who went with him to America. Although an old man at the time of the Revolutionary War, (he) was among the first to raise the sword of freedom for the Colonies.

One Family's Story

Leo B. McDowell and his family make their home in Chancellor, Spotsylvania County, Virginia. Leo's family descends from John Macdowal who was among those family members that fled the Galloway region of Scotland around 1584. In 1595, John Macdowal married Mary Wylie in Gleno, County Antrim, Ulster. These early Ulster-Scot McDowells were kin to the Irvine, Locke, Knox, Blair, Boyd, Lyle, Vans, Fullerton, and Crawford families, just to name a few.

Specifically, Leo is of the southern branch of the family through Robert and Margret McDowell of Mecklenburg, North Carolina, who were among those who came from County Antrim to America in the early 1700s. This family passed through Pennsylvania and Virginia, and eventually settled in colonial North Carolina, having received their initial land grants at the Royal Assembly at New Bern on September 28, 1750.

Leo's sixth great-grandfather Maj. James McDowell commanded 120 North Carolina Volunteers at the Battle of Cowpens in January of 1781 and was cited by the U.S. Congress for providing "heavy and galling fire" against the British forces in that victory. His fifth great-grandfather (Col. William McDowell) fought the Cherokees at the Battle of Dark Hollow and later served with Gen. Thomas "the Gamecock" Sumter.

In 1783, Leo's family was granted land for their service in the American Revolution in western North Carolina. His fourth great-grandfather, John Mc-Dowell, married the former Elizabeth Morrow at the home of his cousins, the McDowells of Pleasant Gardens, Burke (now McDowell) County, North Carolina, in 1799. This Sgt. John McDowell served in the War of 1812 throughout the Carolinas and Georgia.

In 1816, the family removed to the frontier Missouri Territory for a period before returning to Meigs (and later McMinn) County in Tennessee by 1823. By 1850, Leo's family returned to Missouri via covered wagon from Tennessee, with several other related families, to eventually settle in what is now Miller County, Missouri. His great-great-grandfather (William Wilford McDowell) served with Capt. Martin's Company E, Osage County Regiment of the Missouri Home Guard from June through December of 1861.

Leo's grandfather (Robert Harrison McDowell) had been a farmer in Missouri, but later came to Kansas with several brothers to farm, and took work on the railroad around the time of World War I. Leo, his brother (Dr. Richard Lane McDowell), their father (Leo Birtrand McDowell, Sr.), and their grandfather (Robert Harrison McDowell) all worked, at one time or another, for the Missouri Pacific Railroad out of Osawatomie, Miami County, Kansas. During World War II, Leo's uncle Sgt. Wilbert Calvin McDowell served with the Marine's 1st Raider Battalion.

Leo is a Gulf War veteran and retired U.S. Navy cryptologist, and currently serves as a senior intelligence officer for the U.S. Department of Homeland Security. Leo is married to the former Flora Lee Freeman and they have four children and two grandchildren.

Settlement in Early Colonial America

Leo B. McDowell

The earliest known mention in records of any MacDowall in the Americas involves a McDowall of Garthland who is included in the will, dated September 19, 1672, of William Dweare of Barbados and of Calvert County, Maryland, which was probated August 29, 1673.

Several MacDowalls of Garthland served the crown in the West Indies. Col. William MacDowall of the British Army served in St. Christophers, West Indies, where he acquired a considerable plantation. He purchased the ancient barony of Castlesemple in the parish of Lochwinnoch, Renfrewshire, from the eleventh Lord Sempill in 1727, and other baronies.

James McDowell and Elizabeth McDowell Hardy

James McDowell and Elizabeth McDowell of Ireland were recorded as living in the Isle of Wight, Virginia, by the late 1600s. Elizabeth was the wife of the English Capt. Thomas Hardy.

Fergus McDowell of Stonington

Another of the earliest McDowells in America was a Fergus McDowell, an "Irishman" and merchant in Stonington, Connecticut (settled in 1649). This Fergus received a power of attorney from his father-in-law, Ezekiel Cleasby of Boston, Massachusetts, on December 26, 1692. Stonington is on Long Island Sound, near present-day New London and Groton, Connecticut, and at that time was a busy American seaport and a major shipbuilding and whaling center. Fergus may have required the power of attorney to facilitate his business dealings as a merchant. The record of Fergus' power of attorney is in the Suffolk County registry of deeds.

Fergus and his wife Mary Cleasby McDowell had at least three children. Their son James was recorded as living in Stonington, Connecticut, in 1723. Fergus and Mary also had two daughters, Anna and Mary, both of whom married into the Chesebrough family.

Elihu and William Chesebrough were descendants of the prominent Chesebrough family of England and early New England. Anna McDowell (born 1690) married Elihu Chesebrough (born 3 December 1668), the only son of Elisha (born 4 June 1637) and Rebecca Palmer Chesebrough. After Elihu's death in 1671, Anna married John Baldwin of New London on July 24, 1672.

Mary McDowell married William Chesebrough on December 13, 1698, his second wife. William was the son of Samuel Chesebrough (born April 1, 1627), whose first wife Priscilla Alden was the granddaughter of John Alden of the Mayflower. Samuel was the grandson of a William (born c.1594) and Ann Stevenson Chesbrough (married December 15, 1620) of England and the son of Nathaniel Chesbrough (born April 4, 1666) of Boston. William and Mary Chesbrough had five children: William, David, Thomas, Abigail, and Mary.

Anna McDowell Chesebrough Baldwin died in 1725 (age 35) and Mary McDowell Chesebrough died on March 23, 1744.

McDowell Brothers of New Jersey and Pennsylvania

The brothers Alexander, John, and William McDowell immigrated to America by 1718, perhaps as early as 1714–15. Both Alexander and John were described as mariners and surveyors in early Pennsylvania records. Alexander McDowell is listed as a land purchaser on Pennland along the Peapack on the Raritan in Somerset County, New Jersey, along with the Pettinger and many Dutch families. John and Alexander are referred to as brothers in New Jersey, Pennsylvania, and Delaware records. By 1721 both John and Alexander owned property in New Castle County, Delaware.

John was the father of Charles, Robert, William, and Joseph McDowell of Pennsylvania, Virginia, and North Carolina. Two other sons, James and John, Jr., died young in Pennsylvania. James' widow, Mary, moved her family to join the brothers in North Carolina. John died in 1736.

John, Alexander, and William had another brother, Ephraim, who came to America later, by 1731. John's son Robert (born 1709) joined Ephraim and his family on their journey down to Virginia and received land headrights with them in 1737. Robert did not stay in Virginia, but returned to Pennsylvania before finally joining his own brothers Charles, William, and Joseph (and brother James' widow Mary) in Anson County, North Carolina in 1750. Although brother Joseph received his grants in Anson County, North Carolina, in 1750, he did not join his brothers there permanently until about 1762–63.

The elder William (brother of John, Ephraim, and Alexander) and wife Mary Irvine McDowell first settled in Chester County, Pennsylvania, before moving to Wright's Ferry on the Susquehanna River. William's son Col. John McDowell (born c.1715) of Peter's Township, Lancaster County, Pennsylvania, built McDowell's Mill— famous in frontier history as McDowell's Fort—near Bridgeport during the French and Indian War.

Fateful Voyage of the *George and Anne*

One group of McDowells voyaged to America in 1729 on the ship *George and Anne*. At best, such a trip lasted two to three weeks; however, on this occasion, the *George and Anne* took nearly 4½ months. At least 86 souls, of a total of 168 passengers, lost their lives on that voyage, including 12 members of the McDowell family. The ship was overloaded with people, the rations were short or just barely enough, the food was vermin-ridden, and the water was stagnant. The following describes a rather severe ocean voyage of the period and is not atypical; the voyage of the *George and Anne* was even worse.

> The ship—*Sully*—set sail for Philadelphia on the 31st of May and at first was blown off course northward. The weather turned very cold and icebergs were sighted. By the 10th of August, the weather had turned very warm and rations were down to 1 ½# of bread per passenger per week. Two weeks later, the ration was cut further. In the next 12 days, they were reduced to 2 biscuits per week. Hunger and thirst reduced the passengers to shadows. Many killed themselves by drinking salt water or their own urine. They were saved only by a providential rain. On September 2nd, they finally sighted land. This journey had lasted 14 weeks or 3½ months.

The passengers of the *George and Anne* were mostly friends and neighbors from County Longford in Northern Ireland, supplemented by a few last-minute additions in Dublin. The organizer of the expedition was Charles Clinton. The passengers were nearly all free people who paid their own way to go to the land they perceived as offering a better opportunity. They intended to arrive in Pennsylvania, but actually landed on Cape Cod—after a horrendous 4½-month voyage in which most of them perished.

Mr. Clinton kept a journal (or diary) of the voyage, which states that his journey began from the County of Longford on Friday, May 9. He and his family arrived next at Dublin on May 12 and boarded the *George and Anne* on May 18, with the ship getting underway from Dublin on May 20. On the River Liffey in Dublin, just above the O'Connell Street Bridge and about one mile from the ingress of the Irish Sea, the *George and Anne* set sail for America. The ship next arrived at anchor at Glenarm (County Antrim) on May 24, departing the next day. On May 26, the ship came to anchor at Green Castle in the Lough of Foyle, where it remained until May 29, then set sail in the company of the *John of Dublin* bound for Newcastle, Ireland.

The ship caught sight of Loughsuly (Lough Swilly) on May 30, and sailed past Tory Island and Hornhead, bound for America. That night a strong wind arose and continued through the evening of June 1. The wind loosened the bowsprit, hazarding the masts. On June 2, the ship caught a fair breeze and set a westerly course. Clinton's daughter Catherine and son James fell sick with the measles on June 3, and this marks the beginning of an epidemic that would claim the lives of many of the children on board.

The winds continued westerly through June 5, when the first child died. On June 7, the *George and Anne*, presumably still in company with the *John of Dublin*, met the ship *Mary* from Pennsylvania, from which she had sailed in five weeks and five days. On May 8, a child of James McDowell died and its body was committed to the deep. Two days later, the winds had come to east and were now southerly, turning more easterly the next day. On June 12, the winds blew north and east—a fresh gale by which they sailed 40 leagues in 20 hours and found that the ship was at position 49 degrees 20 minutes north latitude by observation.

At this point, additional passengers and their servants began dying at a rate of at least one a day, with additional children becoming ill and succumbing to the measles epidemic. Conditions deteriorated rapidly, with one instance of a servant throwing himself over the side and drowning. On June 17, the winds came to the south with a violent gale, driving the ship off its westerly course and farther south.

According to the ship's journal, on June 12 the *George and Anne* was on a direct northern course from Ireland to Pennsylvania, but by June 21 the reading puts them far south of the Azores in the region of the Canary Islands, off the northwest coast of Africa. This indicates that Captain Rhymer, the ship's master, was incompetent either of determining his position or of maintaining his course. The stated position is well south in the horse latitudes, the area of the Atlantic where sailing ships risked lying motionless adrift, without benefit of wind for long periods.

In the journal entry for the June 21, the ship was in a perfect calm (no wind) at position 27 degrees 30 minutes north latitude. On July 28, the winds turned favorable with a west by northwest heading. The journal continues recording the deaths of the passengers on board through July 7 including the death of another child of James McDowell on that date. Just two days prior they had sighted the Azores at 40 degrees 09 minutes north latitude, 32 degrees 33 minutes west longitude. On July 7, Clinton's journal is no longer being kept and falls silent. By this time multiple deaths were occurring every day.

Apparently there was a long hiatus in Clinton's journal from July 4 to October 4. Prior to this point, Mr. Clinton listed 16 deaths. In the record that followed, he listed 78 deaths (some apparently duplicated from the first list). Perhaps Mr. Clinton was sick, or perhaps there was dissension and thoughts of mutiny on board such that he was too busy to continue the diary during this period.

In the later "Recapitulations," it appears that a total of 80 or 85 died during the voyage. There was a measles epidemic on board, and probably some of the children succumbed to this. Also, in a 4½-month voyage, it was routine in those days for many to die of scurvy (lack of vitamin C). However, most of the deaths on this long voyage of the *George and Anne* were probably due to the incredible overcrowding and inevitable spoilage of food in four months, with fatal diarrhea and vomiting.

For example, Christopher Columbus' *Santa Maria* in 1492 was about the same size (100 tons gross weight, compared to 90 tons for the *George and Anne*) but carried only 50 people on its voyage of little more than two months (compared to an apparent load of 168 passengers plus an unknown number of crew on the *George and Anne*).

As the *George and Anne* was a chartered ship, it was stuffed with as many passengers as possible to collect as many fares as possible. The ship finally reached landfall off the continent of America on October 14, 1729, on Cape Cod. Some accounts indicate that the actual anchorage of the *George and Anne* in America was off Momoloy Island, of the county of Barnstable, Massachusetts. After wintering there, many of the surviving passengers migrated to the Little Britain (Orange County) part of New York. This settlement was located on the western shore of the Hudson River about 60 miles north of New York City.

Another document about the voyage relates:

> On the 20th of May, 1729, the ship left Ireland. After being at sea for some time it was discovered that the Captain (Rhymer) had formed a design of starving his passengers to death, either with the view to obtain their property or to deter emigration. Several of the passengers actually died, among whom were a son and daughter of Mr. Clinton. In this awful situation it was proposed by the passengers to seize the captain and commit the navigation of the vessel to Mr. Clinton, who was an excellent mathematician; but the officers of the ship refusing to co-operate with them, they were deterred from this proceeding from the apprehension of incurring the charge of piracy. They were finally compelled to commute with the captain for their lives by paying a large sum of money; who, accordingly, landed them at Cape Cod on the 4th of October. Mr. Clinton and his friends continued in that part of the country until the spring of 1730, when they removed to the county of Ulster, in the province of New York, and formed a flourishing settlement called Little Britain.

Yet another document relates:

> At last it was discovered by Col. Clinton that it was
> intentionally caused by the Captain, to starve out the
> passengers and lessen their number by death or otherwise, and
> thus possess himself of their money, of which there was
> considerable on board. The captain was seized, put in irons by
> the passengers, and the command given to the mate, who
> brought the ship in, in a few days.

Members of the McDowell Family
on board the *George and Anne*
(18 family members, plus 1 companion)

Group 1: The James McDowell Family

James McDowell (survivor)
Margery McDowell (wife of James, died at sea)
Matthew McDowell (survivor)
Patrick McDowell (died at sea)
Margaret McDowell (died at sea)
Margery McDowell (daughter of James, died at sea)
George McDowell (died at sea)
Sarah McDowell (died at sea)

Group 2: The Andrew McDowell Family

Andrew McDowell, Jr. (survivor, later married Martha
  Giverans of Westchester County, New York)
Elinor McDowell (wife of Andrew, survivor, who died
  a few years later)
James McDowell (survivor)
Mary McDowell (died at sea)
William McDowell (died at sea)
Jean McDowell (died at sea)
Sarah McDowell (died at sea)
Margaret McDowell (died at sea)
Boy McDowell (brother of Andrew, died at sea)

Group 3: John McDowell and Traveling Companion

John McDowell (died at sea)
Thomas Cowin (died at sea)

The accompanying ship *John of Dublin* presumably continued its voyage and arrived at Philadelphia in 1729. Additional members of the McDowell family may have been on board the *John of Dublin*, as well as related Campbells, Irvines, Mitchells, and McElroys.

The Palatine Germans who emigrated to America during the same period on board the same British ships tell of the disembarkation process at their destination:

> First the ones who could pay full price were allowed to pay
> and get off the boat. Next the healthy ones were sold (for
> indentured service) to their new masters for the full fee. Then
> the unhealthy ones were sold at auction. This process often
> took several weeks. If one of the family died (during the
> voyage), the rest of the family members were held accountable
> for passage fees of the deceased.

Despite all this, the Scots-Irish, like the Germans, thought they had found the Promised Land. But by the end of the first half of the 18th century, the peaceful coexistence of Palatine German and Scots-Irish immigrants wore thin. Both held firm to their respective European cultural traditions and social and religious mores. In fact, by 1743 coexistence was no longer possible in cohabited parts of Pennsylvania as reflected by this account:

> The proprietaries, in consequence of the frequent disturbances
> between the governor and Irish [Scots-Irish] settlers, after the
> organization of York and Cumberland counties, gave orders to
> their agents to sell no lands in either York and Lancaster
> counties to the Irish; and also to make advantageous offers of
> removal to the Irish settlers on Paxton and Swatara, and
> Donegal townships, to remove to Cumberland county, which
> offers being liberal, were accepted by many [including some
> McDowells].

Andrew McDowell of the *George and Anne*

Andrew McDowell, of the *George and Anne*, lived for a time in Philadelphia but eventually settled near Nottingham, Chester County, Pennsylvania, where he was recruited as the lieutenant colonel of the 2nd Pennsylvania Battalion of the Colonial Troops in June, 1759. Andrew was related in some close manner to the McDowells of Monmouth and Somerset Counties of New Jersey, including both Alexander and John McDowell (two of the "McDowell Brothers of New Jersey and Pennsylvania" described earlier). Andrew was also related to Ephraim McDowell of Virginia. A list of Andrew and his descendants, probably drawn from the pages of a family Bible and written in the first person singular by Andrew McDowell, with names and birth/death dates can be found in the personal papers of Gov. James McDowell of Virginia, indicating a family connection to Ephraim's family.

It is this author's contention that Andrew was most likely a son of Alexander McDowell who owned land on Peapack in Somerset County, New Jersey, and ancestor of the McDowells of Perth Amboy, New Jersey. Since Alexander was a brother of Ephraim McDowell of Virginia, this would explain the interest and connection to Ephraim and his descendants.

McDowells of Virginia and Kentucky

Linda McDowell Swann

Among the first McDowells known to have arrived and lived in Virginia were James McDowell and Elizabeth McDowell of Ireland, undoubtedly Ulster. She was the wife of Capt. Thomas Hardy. They are recorded as living in Isle of Wight, Virginia, in the late 1600s. Isle of Wight was located not far from Jamestown and the Norfolk region that gradually spread from the original settlement along the James River.

It was not until the first half of the next century that the great wave of Scots and Scots-Irish began to arrive along the eastern seaboard of the British colonies. Whether or not it was the deliberate policy of the early King Georges to buffer their more profitable sea coast lands from the Indians with the fierce and often intractable North Britons, their fighting abilities had swelled the ranks of the British Army; and conditions, particularly in Northern Ireland, had proved that the land and religious freedom they hungered for was not to be theirs for the taking in Ireland. Recruiters and land agents ranged the ports of Ulster offering land and opportunity to those willing to risk their lives and families for a chance in the New World.

Ephraim McDowell

Ephraim McDowell, born in 1672 and founder of the Virginia and Kentucky dynasty whose family roots have been traced back to the McDowalls of Garthland in Galloway, was only one of the Ulstermen McDowells who as an older man decided to uproot himself and those of his children willing to take ship for America. The movement of Gallovidians to whom Ireland was so close had gone on for untold centuries. Even the mother of Robert the Bruce was a Gallovidian and his second wife the daughter of the Earl of Ulster. The religious troubles of the century before King James I of England and VI of Scotland decided to repopulate Catholic Ireland with his troublesome Scots had added to the tide. Ephraim as a young boy in his teens had fought for the Protestant William of Orange at both the Battle of the Boyne in 1688 and at the siege of Londonderry. Now he was no longer willing to stay in Ulster after the death of his wife Margaret Irvine and decided to emigrate to the colonies. The exact number of his children is not known, but some elected to stay in County Antrim.

It is generally believed that Ephraim, his sons James and John, and daughters Mary Elizabeth and Margaret sailed on the *George and Anne* in 1729 with his nephews and nieces, the children of his brother Andrew who had been in Philadelphia as early as 1725. Other McDowells along with Irvines sailed on a sister ship the *John of Dublin*. The *George and Anne* had a hellish voyage, on which several McDowells died, eventually landing at Cape Cod after an agonizing four and a half months before proceeding to Pennsylvania, while the *John of Dublin* made it to Philadelphia as planned. Confusion over the passenger lists is understandable with the Christian names shared not only among the McDowells but, it seems, every other immigrating family of that period.

Ephraim's family is known to have reached Pennsylvania, settling there for a few years before deciding to move south to the Valley of Virginia. Their kinsman John Lewis had by 1732 settled on the headwaters of the Shenandoah; his holding "Bellfont" was near today's town of Staunton. Ephraim's son James McDowell went first, planting a crop of corn by the spring of 1737. That summer Ephraim moved again, with his son John together with his wife Magdalene Woods, daughter of Michael Woods and Mary Campbell, who settled in what was to be Albemarle County. Also moving were Ephraim's daughter Mary Elizabeth who had married James Greenlee, John's son Samuel, and John's indentured servant John Rutter.

September found the little party in the Valley; one evening when they had pulled off the "Indian Road" to camp by Linville Creek in what is now Rockingham County, they were joined by another group of travelers whose fortunes from that day were to be joined with them for life. The leader of the second party was Benjamin Borden, a former agent of Lord Fairfax, who was traveling to take possession and develop a grant that had been given him. The purpose of his mission was to find settlers for 100,000 acres. He hoped for a hundred families who would take up land across the frontier in the grand plan of the English proprietors. Perhaps he had a map, but not being familiar with the territory, Borden offered a thousand acres to whoever could guide him to his holding and establish the measure and bounds of his land. Around the campfire, John McDowell, hearing this, informed Borden that he was a surveyor and by the light of a torch showed him his instruments. A bargain was struck and made formal with papers drawn the next day when the conjoined party reached Lewis's "Bellfont."

Sept. ye 19th 1737

This day John McDowell of Orange County in Virginia have agreed with Benjamin Borden of the same place that he the said McDowell would go now with his family and his father and his Brothers and make four Settlements in the same Bordens land which was granted to the said Borden on this side of the blue ridge in the fork of the said River, and said McDowell has agreed with the said Borden that he the sd

McDowell would cut a good Road for Horses loaded with common Luggage and blaze the Trees all the way plain and also the said McDowell has agreed with the said Benjamin Borden that he the said McDowell would go with the sd Borden and take account of the Settlement of Borden Land on the River called the Chimbly Stone and on Smith Creek and be evidence for the said Borden of all his settlements aforesaid, and in consideration of the premises the said Borden is to give one thousand acres of Land when he the said McDowell build in the sd fork of the sd River and the sd Borden is to give the said McDowell good lawfull Deed as the said Borden can get of the King clear of all charges excepting the quitrents & also the said Borden do here agree to given to these the other three Settlements six hundred acres of Land clear of all charges as before excepted and the said McDowell is to go down with a compt (count) of all the Settlements as aforesaid with Borden to his House by the tenth day of October next to go with said Borden to Colo Willis to price the Settlements as aforesaid as witness my hand

BENJAMIN BORDEN

John (Ephraim's Son)

Next, the party traveled through the southern boundary of Beverley Manor to the headwaters of the James. Camping on a spring branch that led to the river and determining that it flowed south, they knew they had come to Borden's Grant. Here John McDowell built a cabin on land that later came into the possession of Andrew Scott, the first house in what was to be Rockbridge County. Borden wanted McDowell to take his land on Hays Creek, but McDowell, knowing the lay of the land better, was firm that he wanted to be on Timber Ridge. This land was on the upland overlooking the South River valley along what was to be built as the "Pennsylvania Road," now U.S. Route 11 and paralleled by Interstate 81. This proved to be the main artery of migration south along the Valley to southwestern Virginia, the Carolinas, Kentucky, and Tennessee.

Whether it was John McDowell or his strong-willed wife Magdalene who determined that their home was to be different from the other log cabins of their neighbors is not known, but John McDowell took the red ochre clay for which Virginia is famous and stripped and covered his logs with the mixture to make his home the "Red House." The fine brick mansion that stands in its place today still bears the name. It was probably in the Red House that the later two children of John and Magdalene were born. Their son Samuel, born in 1735, had been "imported into the colony" with them and their servant John Rutter, as recorded at the Orange County Court in 1739. James was born in 1739 and Sarah was born in the summer and baptized by the Rev. John Craig on a visit from the Tinkling Springs Presbyterian Church in October of 1741.

By 1742, John McDowell had been named a captain of the impromptu militia that more or less included the able-bodied men of the settlement who stood ready to defend their holdings from whatever threats appeared. In late 1742, a band of 30 Iroquois warriors traveled en route from Onondaga to the Catawba nation, with passes from the white authorities that had not been ratified for Virginia. Since hunting was scarce, the Indians soon fell on the settlers' livestock, even to the point of shooting arrows into their horses, thus raising the alarms and fears of the community. When he was informed of this, Col. James Patton, the County Lieutenant, sent word to Capt. John McDowell ordering him to locate and escort the Indians out of the county of Augusta, which at that time constituted much of the area of the Blue Ridge and the Valley.

There were only 39 names on the roster of the company and they were scattered far and wide, but word was sent out for them to muster at the Red House. In the meantime, the Indians under Chief Jonnhaty of the Onondaga had arrived at the Red House seeking food, but they were concerned over the increasing numbers of white men they saw. Some of the older Indians actually went into the house but the others, becoming more apprehensive, resisted being confined and feared a trap. An attempt was made to keep the Indians there, but with the chief urging them to let the whites make the first move, the band moved out and went back to the valley of the South River.

On December 18, one of the settlers came upon the Indian camp and, taking count of their number, reported to the Red House. Captain McDowell decided he would try to obey Colonel Patton's request and move the Indians on their way. He assembled his men, reportedly among them his father Ephraim and his brother James. They met the band and were in the process of accompanying them past the Salling lands—the farthest reaches of the settlement—when a lame Indian fell behind and one of the settlers shot at him. A fierce fight broke out near Balcony Falls on a creek that came to be called Battle Run creek, and John McDowell was one of the first to fall. Accounts vary as to whether it was eight or nine of the settlers who fell with him, but 17 of the Indians were also killed.

The bodies of the settlers were brought back dangling across their saddles to the Red House, where Magdalene McDowell helped prepare her husband and the other men for burial. The family plot was selected a little to the north of the house (the Timber Ridge Presbyterian meeting house now lies about a mile south). Strong in her faith, Magdalene, no doubt, saw that services were conducted for the fallen. Today, the plot is filled with early relatives of the McDowells and, although overgrown, is marked with a historical marker commemorating Capt. John McDowell's early sacrifice.

Magdalene (John's Widow)

Ephraim McDowell had taken up 300 acres near his son John's home and in 1755 sold it to his son James. This was his home and it was no doubt with his help that Magdalene McDowell, left with three young children, was able to keep her lands and rear them. Ephraim's daughter Margaret had married John Mitchell, son of John and Mary Boyd Mitchell, and they also lived nearby. As earlier noted, Ephraim's other daughter Mary Elizabeth had married James Greenlee and, like her father, lived past 100 years of age.

According to Peyton's history of Rockbridge County, some of Mary's neighbors reputed her long life to dark powers. Certainly, she was a strong and forceful character. At one point, she was asked to try to win back a daughter of the Lewis family, her kinsmen, who they believed had been taken by the Indians. Since the Indians trusted Mary more than most whites, she was able to go to their camp and discover what happened. She found the girl and learned some element of romance with a young brave had lured her off but persuaded her to return to her family, demanding as payment the horse the girl came back on.

Mary's daughter Grizzell or Grace married her cousin Charles McDowell of Quaker Meadows in North Carolina, whose family had also started out in the Valley of Virginia. Grace, too, gave birth to a long line of judges, senators, lawyers, and distinguished men and women. As an old woman, Mary's help was sought in establishing early land boundaries and her recall was considered remarkable for its clarity and exactness. One episode where she did not come off so well concerns an erstwhile poet who told her he would write her epitaph in exchange for a bottle of whiskey. His first installment pleased her, reading:

> Good old Mary died of late,
> Straight she went to Heaven's gate.

This sounded promising so she gave him the whiskey, but then he drank it and continued:

> But Abraham met her with a club
> And knocked her back to Beelzebub!

Infuriated, she is said to have chased him out with her broom. Knowing as he did of her reputation as an old witch, it is surprising he did not think she might pursue him *on* it!

Surrounded as she was by such strong characters, it is not so surprising that Magdalene McDowell went on to see her children and children's children achieve prominence and respect in the land she pioneered. She placed Samuel, her eldest, in the classical school taught first by Robert Alexander and then by the Rev. John Brown. He went on, as we shall see, to serve in the American Revolution and become one of the founding fathers of the state of Kentucky. Her second son, James, was the father of the James McDowell who was a governor of Virginia. McDowell, Virginia, in Highland County where Stonewall Jackson won a battle in 1862 and McDowell County in what is now West Virginia are named for him. Her daughter Sarah married Col. George Moffett, a noted Indian fighter and soldier of the Revolution who fought at Guilford, Cowpens, and Kings Mountain, and had nine children. Her children and grandchildren also became noted judges, soldiers, and businessmen.

Magdalene did not remain a widow, but sometime around 1744 married Benjamin Borden, Jr., the son of the man who had made her family's fortune around that fateful campfire. He had come to the Valley as his father's representative to complete titles for land already sold and make deeds for new sales. He stayed for a time at the Red House and, according to Magdalene's sister-in-law Mary Greenlee, did not make a good impression at first. Magdalene, however, might have seen a perfectly respectable 18th century way of solving land disputes through marriage. Benjamin went on to earn the esteem of his neighbors, becoming a County Justice and a Captain of the Augusta Militia. He and Magdalene had two daughters.

In 1746, Magdalene McDowell Borden had continued in her Presbyterian steadfastness, setting her name as a member of the Timber Grove Meeting House; but Borden being a Quaker, like his father, did not sign. In 1753, she was one of three women who signed to call the Rev. John Brown to the Timber Ridge and New Providence churches. But that year, she was to need her faith when disaster struck by way of a smallpox epidemic that carried off Benjamin Borden, Jr., and baby Magdalene in the spring.

Magdalene was now one of the richest women on the frontier, the heiress of the Borden estate. She was a prize for the taking and described as being "tall and straight, handsome with dazzling white skin, big blue eyes, and long yellow hair. A witty tongue, great charm, a dashing determination which carries everything before her, a rather imperious person evidently, but very attractive and much beloved." She is described in an old letter as "riding a famous black stallion in a riding-coat of 'hunter's green' with gold buttons and a bonnet of many plumes." She was undoubtedly pursued, as she did not remain a widow long. This time, though, it was said there not much sentiment on either side when she married John Bowyer, a young schoolmaster reportedly twenty years her junior in 1754. Her sister-in-law Mary McDowell Greenlee remembers him as "ambitious and very aggressive." According to tradition, Magdalene had a marital agreement drawn up to secure her property to herself and her children, which Bowyer threw in the fire. He outlived her and became in his turn a captain and then a colonel in the Militia, but John McDowell's land passed out of the family.

Samuel (John and Magdalene's Son)

Thus, it is not surprising that Samuel McDowell looked west to secure land for himself and his many children. He married another Scots-Irish immigrant from Ireland, Mary McClung. After serving in the French and Indian War, fighting at Point Pleasant as well as under Washington, he served as a colonel in the Revolution, distinguishing himself at Guilford Court House. A surveyor like his father, he was appointed by Washington to survey in Kentucky and as justice for the new territory. He was president of the convention that framed the first constitution of Kentucky and present at the meeting that founded the Transylvania Seminary, which was to become Transylvania University in Lexington. Settling near what is now Danville, he had a long and prominent career in his new state, and his twelve children fanned out to provide further generations of doctors, lawyers, and builders of the American dream.

His son Ephraim, named for his grand-father, was the father of abdominal surgery. He studied medicine with Dr. Humphreys in Staunton, Virginia; completed his advanced medical studies at the University of Edinburgh, Scotland; then went to Danville, Kentucky, to practice. He performed the first operation for the successful removal of an ovarian cyst without anesthetic on a stalwart daughter of the pioneers who lived for many years thereafter. His most famous patient was the future president, James K. Polk, who at the age of 17 in 1812 had gallstones removed and a hernia repaired. Like his father, Dr. Ephraim helped found a college, Centre in Danville. His statue stands in the United States Capitol, donated by the Commonwealth of Kentucky as one of her most famous sons.

National Statuary Hall Collection

Dr. Ephraim McDowell

Also among Samuel's descendants was Gen. Irvin McDowell from the branch that

moved to Ohio, who returned to Virginia only to be defeated at the first
Battle of Bull Run. Although his Army career was damaged by this
defeat, he went on to become a parks commissioner in California and
laid out the roads for the Presidio which overlooks the Golden Gate
Bridge.

Ephraim's family of McDowells are among the most distinguished
and easily traced of the many McDowells who came to Virginia, the
Carolinas, Kentucky, and Tennessee. Interlacing with the descendants of
the two Josephs of Quaker Meadows and Pleasant Gardens, respectively,
in North Carolina by marrying cousins, they are a tribute to the
genealogist's dream and stretch their proud heritage from coast to coast.

Other McDowell Pioneers

Hundreds of other McDowells also struggled from Galloway and
Ireland to America. The *George and Anne, John of Dublin*, and other
ships brought others who, though less noted, nevertheless made their
mark and traveled from New England to Georgia and beyond. The Rev.
Alexander McDowell lived in the regions of early Virginia and served
the congregations of North Mountain, New Providence, Timber Ridge,
and Forks of James. His proximity to Magdalene's family makes it
possible he too was a relative.

Archibald McDowell served as a volunteer in Botetourt County
under Robert McClenachan in 1774. The number of John McDowells
alone in the census of 1800 is truly daunting to the researcher, without
the many variations of the name to McDole, MacDuel, and the like. In
East Kentucky and across the Big Sandy into West Virginia are
numerous pockets of McDowells who have also spread across the nation.

Even before George Washington sent Samuel McDowell to bring the
protection of the federal government to Kentucky, Daniel Boone was
accompanied by a Thomas McDowell, probably from North Carolina,
whose sad end is best told in Boone's own words:

> April 15th, 1775.
>
> Dear Colonel: After my compliments to you, I shall acquaint
> you with our misfortune. On March the 25th a party of Indians
> fired on my company about half an hour before day, and killed
> Mr. Twitty and his negro, and wounded Mr. Walker very
> deeply but I hope he will recover.
>
> On March the 28th, as we were hunting for provisions, we
> found Samuel Tate's son, who gave us an account that the
> Indians fired on their camp on the 27th day. My brother and I
> went down and found two men killed and scalped, Thomas
> McDowell and Jeremiah McPeters. I have sent a man down to

all the lower companies in order to gather them all to the mouth of Otter Creek. My advice to you, sir, is to come or send as soon as possible. Your company is desired greatly, for the people are very uneasy, but are willing to stay and venture their lives with you; and now is the time to flusterate their (the Indians) intentions, and keep the country whilst we are in it. If we give way to them now, it will ever be the case. This day we start from the battle-ground for the mouth of Otter Creek, where we shall immediately erect a fort, which will be done before you can come or send; then we can send ten men to meet you if you send for them.

I am, sir, your most obedient

DANIEL BOONE.

N.B.—We stood on the ground and guarded our baggage till day, and lost nothing. We have about fifteen miles to Cantuck, at Otter Creek.

By 1810, a William McDowell (thought by some to be Samuel's son, though it seems unlikely) was in Floyd County, Kentucky, and was joined by yet another John McDowell there. What their relationship was is not known, but it seems likely they were kinsmen and lived near each other. It is possible they were part of the North Carolina movement to that part of eastern Kentucky, but many others came down the Ohio to the Big Sandy from Virginia and Pennsylvania. That part of Floyd County was later divided to form Lawrence County; there are McDowells still there to this day, though many of them have spread across the country.

Of the McDowells in Lawrence County, Kentucky, one sprang to notoriety in the 1840s. John McDowell was accused of having murdered his wife, Jenny Caines, the daughter of the man for whom Caines Creek near what is now Blaine was named. Further investigation exonerated him and nothing more was heard.

The McDowells continued in the Caines Creek area living in the community of Sacred Wind until one of their number, Joe, moved to nearby Ashland, Kentucky. His son Augusta, born in a log cabin at Sacred Wind, enlisted in the U.S. Army before World War II and was sent to Iceland before war was declared. From there, he was sent to England to train for the invasion of Europe. On leave, he traveled north to Scotland and, searching for his roots, found Garthland, an ancestral home of many McDowells. He was graciously received there and taken on a tour of the estate. Continuing the warrior tradition of the family, he fought from Omaha Beach through the Battle of the Bulge to the occupation of Germany.

After the war, Gus, as he was known, went to work for the Ashland Oil and Refining Company as an engineer on the company's towboats, which plied the Ohio River from Pittsburgh to New Orleans, and invented many modifications for the boats' engines. After a stroke ended his career on the river, he went to work in the research and development section of Ashland Oil. When he retired, he learned of the Gathering of the Clans at Grandfather Mountain in North Carolina and became an enthusiastic member of the Clan MacDougall Society, to which the McDowells belong. As a new member, he eventually ordered a kilt from Scotland, but it was very slow in arriving. Typical of Gus's own brand of dire Scots humor, he finally wrote to the company and told them that if the kilt did not come soon he would be wearing it at his funeral. Sadly, he was nearly right and wore it only once before he was buried in it. His children, Donald, Robin, and Linda, have gone on to be a commercial fisherman, an editor, and a university library cataloger. They have all returned to Virginia and remain active in the Clan MacDougall Society.

The pioneer McDowells and those who came after them helped shape both Virginia and Kentucky from their earliest days to the present. As the country spread west, they were at the forefront of their states' development and added their sons and daughters to the growing glory that became America.

To Virginia and the Carolinas: The Great Wagon Road

Leo B. McDowell

The story of the migration of the McDowells from Scotland and Ireland to the Carolinas and west was produced by pioneers such as McDowell brothers John (born c.1670), Alexander, and William[*] who voyaged to America in the early 1700s, settling first in Monmouth and Somerset Counties in New Jersey. Both John and Alexander were described as mariners in early colonial records, and Alexander and his family ran ships out of Perth Amboy, New Jersey.

Alexander purchased land at Peapack on the Raritan River in Somerset County, New Jersey. John owned land in nearby New Castle County, Delaware. William settled at Parnell's Knob in 1719 and was well known in Chester and Lancaster Counties in Pennsylvania. John's son Robert bought land in Caln and Nottingham townships, also in Chester and Lancaster Counties.

In about 1731 Ephraim McDowell[†] met his brothers in Perth Amboy before continuing westward.

Pennsylvania

The frontier McDowells, like other Scots-Irish families, originally occupied the hills around the settlements in Pennsylvania, such as Carlisle, Caln, Nottingham, Donegal, and Stranbane. When Lancaster County was established on May 10, 1729, it became the prototype for the 63 counties to follow. The original three counties, Philadelphia, Bucks, and Chester, were created as copies of typical English shires.

The frontier conditions of Chester County's backwoods, from which Lancaster was formed, presented knotty problems to the civilized Englishmen. Lancaster County, therefore, was an experiment in pragmatism erected on the periphery of William Penn's "Holy Experiment." Pennsylvania's "first western county" would test the genius of English government and political common sense.

Political control of Pennsylvania at this time rested in the hands of the Quakers. They looked with disfavor on the arrival of the bellicose Scots-Irish, who generally moved toward the frontier and whose contempt for the English was only slightly milder than their hatred of the

---

[*] See "McDowell Brothers of New Jersey and Pennsylvania," page 56.
[†] See "Ephraim McDowell," page 63.

"red savages." A new county might cause competition, for surely the Scots-Irish would demand representation in the Provincial Assembly.

There was also opposition from the Germans. More local government would mean more regulations and higher taxes. Fortunately, on the banks of the Susquehanna River at Wright's Ferry, there existed a settlement of remarkably competent Quaker politicians who adjusted intelligently to the challenges of the frontier, including the Indians and Scots-Irish.

Eight magistrates, all of British ancestry and mostly Quakers, were appointed to subdivide Lancaster County into townships. By August 5, 1729, the settled portions of the county had been organized into 17 townships with names chosen with the usual jockeying for honors. Two celebrated the Welsh (Caernarvon and Lampeter), two had Indian names (Conestoga and Paxtank [Peshtank or Paxton], six were English (Warwick, Lancaster, Martic, Sadsbury, Salisbury and Hempfield), four kept the Scots-Irish happy (Donegal, Drumore, Derry, and Leacock), one was German (Manheim), one came from the Bible (Lebanon), and one was the Anglicization of the family name Graf or Groff (Earl). Late in 1729 an eighteenth township was created: Cocalico, an Indian name.

Lancaster County was entitled to only four representatives in the Provincial Assembly, the three older counties being given six assemblymen each. Initially, each election in the county was a contest between the Scots-Irish and the English Quakers, with new faces appearing only to be defeated the following year. By 1731, however, troubles with the Indians tipped the balance in favor of the rugged Scots-Irish at the expense of the pacifistic Quakers. By 1734 James Hamilton, an Ulsterman and proprietor of Lancaster and the son of the distinguished lawyer Andrew Hamilton, won a seat in the Assembly and became the political leader of the county.

Those Scots-Irish who had indentured themselves to reach America set out for the frontier immediately upon fulfilling their indenture. The other persons of means supplied themselves with the materials required on the frontier: muskets, dried and salted provisions, seed for planting, implements, blankets, etc. The McDowells were of the latter type. In fact, at least one son of Ephraim (John, born 1714) had brought along his servant from Ireland, named John Rutter. This was not an uncommon practice by persons of means. Of course, once in America, the servant could qualify for his own headrights (land grant) when released from service.

The "frontier" was 40 to 50 miles west of Philadelphia, and south in the foothills of the mountains in Western Maryland or along the Chesapeake Bay, the Potomac River, or their tributaries. The frontiersmen marked their property by cutting their initials in trees on the boundary of what they considered to be theirs, then cutting circles in the bark to kill the tree. Some often refused to pay for the land, since they believed God owned it.

Their Scots-Irish language, religion, culture, and customs continued in America. The immigrant wives spun flax, milled the corn, worked in the fields, and often bore 10 to 15 children, for whom the mortality rate was extremely high. They also educated their own children. The Scots-Irish felled trees and cleared around the stumps, rather than clearing the land properly, as the German immigrants had learned to do.

Homemade whiskey was important for trade and made a harsh life more tolerable. A common item on a Scots-Irishman's farm was a still, and distilleries sprang up along many of the plantations. One account of the 1840s era reported six distilleries in the neighborhood. "Brown Betty," as the product was often called, was a common item at weddings and other social events. The Gaelic word *ceilidh* fits for this type of social event—music, dancing, singing, drinking, and socializing.

The church was the mainstay of the early settlers' social life. Little contact was made with the neighbors, except in the churchyard on Sundays. All of the early churches were Presbyterian (Associate Reformed Presbyterian included). The Scots-Irish were known for drinking, arguing, singing, and dancing, but neighbors gathered to clear land, build houses, harvest crops, and then hold the ceilidh.

The Scots-Irish were used unknowingly to form a cordon around the English and the Germans. The Germans were settled a little farther inland than the English to provide a buffer between the English and the Indians, and the Scots-Irish were settled a bit farther into the frontier than even the Germans. This was another example of the English solving two problems at once.

It was recorded that for every Indian killed, 50 Scots-Irish settlers were either killed or kidnapped by Indians, and a kind of moral bankruptcy took place in the Scots-Irish that would be termed racist genocide today. The Scots-Irish continued their movement down the Cumberland, along the Blue Ridge into Virginia and the Shenandoah Valley, and down into the Carolinas.

Conowingo, Maryland

In 1731 Charles, his wife Rachel, and his family left Pennsylvania, traveled down the Susquehanna River into Maryland, and joined other McDowells there, including William and Ruth Ann Roberts McDowell. Charles and Rachel lingered for a time, growing corn in the Conowingo settlement in Cecil County, Maryland. Conowingo is situated on what was once the hunting grounds of the Susquesahanocks, members of an Iroquois-speaking tribe who followed the course of the Susquehanna in their fishing and trading expeditions. The great river, which bounds Conowingo on the west, was for centuries a natural artery for travel. The Indians established a palisaded village at the mouth of the Octoraro Creek near an area known to the Indians as Conewago or Conowingo, which in the language of the Susquesahanocks meant "at the rapids."

Captain John Smith left records of his exploratory voyage from Jamestown in 1608, to a point only a few miles downstream from Conowingo, where falls in the river (now known as Smith's Falls) made further passage of his ship impossible. The first settler in the area was an Englishman by the name of Richard Hall, who is supposed to have arrived in 1640. The river hills soon after became peopled with other pioneers, for there are numerous abodes that date back to colonial days. These early settlers were farmers, fishermen, and slaveholders that included the Cathey and McDowell families. The settler men were of English or Scots-Irish stock, and the early churches were Quaker and Presbyterian. The Cathey family had lived in Conowingo, Cecil County, Maryland, as early as 1719. It is possible that Charles McDowell's wife Rachel was a member of this Cathey family. Members of the Cathey family continued to live alongside the McDowells in Virginia, South and North Carolina, and Tennessee for several generations.

Virginia

John Lewis, the son of Andrew and Mary Calhoun Lewis of Donegal and a close kinsman to the McDowells, founded the Augusta settlement in the Shenandoahs in 1732.

The McDowells had aided John Lewis in fleeing Ulster to America. A bounty of 50 pounds sterling was placed on him for his capture after he killed his Irish Laird (landlord) Campbell.

It seems that the young laird, the son of Laird Mingho Campbell, saw that John Lewis was prosperous, and decided that Lewis' rent on his estate should be increased. He went to Lewis' house with several hired ruffians, but was rebuffed and refused entry. He attempted to break in but failed, so one of his group fired a musket through the view ports of Lewis' home, mortally wounding Lewis' sick and bedridden brother. The same musket ball also struck the hand of John Lewis' wife Margaret.

Lewis flew into a rage, grabbed his shillelagh, and "clefted the Laird's skull in half, spilling brains and blood all about," killing him instantly. The McDowells, Calhouns, Kyles, MacLarrans, and other kinsmen sided with Lewis in this affair and provided him safe hiding until he could escape from Ireland to America. The MacLarrans and Kyles were kin to the McDowells from the days back in Scotland.

The opening of William Beverly's Manor on the headwaters of the Shenandoah River and the granting to Benjamin Borden of a patent to a large tract of land in Frederick County on the Shenandoah, known as "Borden's Manor," lured many Scots-Irish settlers discontented with events in Pennsylvania.

Among the problems: the Penn Proprietaries decided that some occupants of lands in Lancaster County should be relocated to new lands farther west to make way for a large estate in the Lancaster area. In addition, many Scots-Irish were rankled by the refusal of some of their Dutch Quaker neighbors to condone any self-defense against the Indians. For those and other reasons, the Scots-Irish settlers were ready to answer the call to the Valley of Virginia.

Often, a member of the family moved to the valley, located a tract, engaged it, and returned to Pennsylvania for the other members of his family. They and other neighbors, impressed by reports of the new lands, formed a caravan heading for the Virginia frontier.

Thus, in 1736 James McDowell came in advance to the South River in the Shenandoah Valley of Virginia and planted corn in the valley opposite Woods Gap. Then in September 1737, Ephraim McDowell (already an old man of nearly 65 years), his sons John and James, his daughter Mary Elizabeth McDowell Greenlee, and her husband James Greenlee moved there from Pennsylvania and Maryland. They were accompanied by Ephraim's nephew Robert, who would return to Pennsylvania later for his family. These McDowells had come out of County Antrim sailing from Larne or Belfast with their kin, the families McElroy, McCune, McCampbell, McKee, Moffett, and Irvine (the family of Ephraim's wife).

Ephraim's family journeyed down what was sometimes called the Indian Road, Great Wagon, or Pennsylvania Road and stopped to camp on Linville (or Linn's) Creek in Orange (now Rockingham) County, Virginia. Just after the McDowells established their camp, Benjamin Borden arrived and spent the night with them. He told them he had received a grant from King George of 100,000 acres of land along the waters of the James River, provided he could find it. To the man who would show him the boundaries, Borden would give 1000 acres. Ephraim's son John replied that he was a surveyor and would accept the offer.[*]

Ephraim, his son John, and his nephew Robert were all present at the Orange County Virginia Court of Common Pleas on February 28, 1739, to receive their Virginia headrights. Headrights were grants of 50 acres of land per "head" (or per white male over the age of 16) to those men who transported themselves to the colonies. By this reckoning, (provided

---

[*] For the contract between John McDowell and Borden, see page 64 in the "McDowells of Virginia and Kentucky" chapter.

his sons James and William were over 16 years old) Robert McDowell was entitled to 150 acres of land in Orange County, Virginia. The Scots-Irish chose lands in America that closely resembled the areas in Northern Ireland from which they had come. They preferred the rolling hills and highlands of the Appalachian and Blue Ridge Mountains and the fertile Cumberland and Shenandoah Valleys of Pennsylvania and Virginia.

Back in Pennsylvania

Another John McDowell (not Robert's father), probably a son of Alexander McDowell of Perth Amboy, became a mariner and captain of the ship *Jolly Bachelor*. John died on board his ship at Cape Fear, in Brunswick County, North Carolina, in 1735. John left his property to his brother James, sister Jane McDowell Nesbit, and a friend, Lydia Jones. He also gave a legacy of 10 pounds to his uncle, John McDowell of New Castle County, Delaware; 10 pounds to the Presbyterian church in Dover, Delaware; and five pounds to the Episcopal church in Dover. He wished that a "small brick wall be put around (my) grave with two marble stones set up, one at the head and one at the foot, as is commonly used in such cases at Philadelphia."

Robert returned to Pennsylvania from Virginia, possibly upon receiving news of his father's death. John McDowell died October 17, 1738, and is buried at Christ Church burial ground (resting place of Benjamin Franklin) in Philadelphia, Pennsylvania.

John's death in 1738 triggered a new migration of his family members. By 1750 Robert and his family moved to Anson County, North Carolina, joining Charles McDowell, "Hunting" John McDowell, Mary McDowell, and Joseph McDowell in receiving their grants at the Royal Assembly at New Bern.

North and South Carolina

In mid-century, Charles and Rachel McDowell and their son John's family moved from Winchester, traveling down the Shenandoah Valley to Anson County, North Carolina. Charles had received a grant for 200 acres on the Broad River in Anson County on April 4, 1751.

Charles's son, Hunting John McDowell, received a grant of 640 acres on the south side of the Broad River on a branch of Little River on November 18, 1752. He later sold the 640 acres to James Harris for 16 pounds 5 shillings.

Charles died in May 1754 and left 10 pounds local currency to his son John, while the daughters received equal portions of the estate. Charles's wife received one-third of the estate and the property in present-day Cherokee County, South Carolina. The land on the Broad

River, which was bequeathed to Rachel McDowell Eagan, was later sold by Rachel and her husband, Barnaby S. Eagan. Their attorney was Charles's great-grandson, John McDowell of Haywood County.

Charles' will, written on January 24, 1754, stipulated that his brother Joseph McDowell of Frederick (Orange) County, Virginia, was to receive "one brown broad cloth coat, one beaver hat, and one pair of snow boots." These garments were handsome in that day, and denoted high social standing and wealth.

Charles was reportedly buried in McDowell Cemetery at Quaker Meadows. However, other sources indicate he is buried on land that he owned in what is now Cherokee County, South Carolina.

From History of the McDowells and Connections, *by John Hugh McDowell*
Quaker Meadows in 1918.

Joseph and his family also relocated to North Carolina after selling their land in Winchester in 1763. The land Joseph later owned in North Carolina became the plantations of McDowell Station at Quaker Meadows. Hunting John's land became Pleasant Gardens, while Pennsylvanian James McDowell's son John (born 1743) owned the land later known as Cleghorn Estate.

On September 16, 1764, the Crown Governor of North Carolina patented to Col. John McDowell (born 1743) a tract of land in what was then Mecklenburg County. This is the first recorded history of the domain of the Cleghorn Plantation on Cleghorn Creek and Broad River. This John McDowell was the son of James McDowell (born 1707, died 1747 in Pennsylvania) of Derry Township, Lancaster County, Pennsylvania. As mentioned, James's widow Mary had brought her children to North Carolina after James's death. Mary and members of her family, including Col. John and his wife, Jane Parks McDowell, are buried in the Steel Creek Presbyterian Church cemetery in Mecklenburg County.

Charles and Hunting John McDowell and their families were among the first settlers in North Carolina's Burke, McDowell, Rowan, and Anson Counties. Also present receiving grants in Anson County was Mary, the widow of Charles's brother, James McDowell. Mary took their children and joined the McDowells in North Carolina. Also joining Charles were three other brothers: Robert (born 1709, later of Mecklenburg County), William (born 1711, also of Mecklenburg County), and Joseph (born 1715, later of Quaker Meadows). They all received their Royal Grants in Anson County from the Royal Executive Sessions at New Bern, North Carolina, in 1750–51. No doubt having traveled there together, their individual grants lay along the various creeks and tributaries of Rocky River.

Quaker Meadows and Pleasant Gardens later became the McDowell plantation estates in old Burke County. The earliest settlers in North Carolina, in what is now Rutherford County (originally made up from parts of Burke and Anson Counties) probably came there around 1730. These early settlers of North Carolina were primarily German and the Scots-Irish.

Throughout the mountains the majority were the Scots-Irish, like those that settled in the Cane Creek area and later formed Brittain Church. Tory pressure during the Revolutionary War forced the family of Robert McDowell (born 1709) to move farther north to Dutch Buffalo Creek in Mecklenburg County from Anson County when. His son Maj. James (born c.1730) and grandson William (born 1748) moved west into what is now Haywood County (old Buncombe County) in 1783 after the removal of the Cherokee. William's son, John McDowell (born 1774) of Haywood County lived at Flowery Gardens and was also the owner of "Kaintucky Bottoms" near Cane Creek.

These Scots-Irish brought their own ordained ministers with them. The Presbyterian ministers were college-trained and served also as educators. Many of the settlers were or became educated, and could read their own Bibles. The Presbyterians elected their own church elders, in sharp contrast to the hierarchy of the Catholic Church.

Hunting John McDowell took out a land grant in 1748 from Swan's Pond up the Catawba River to Garden City and Buck Creek. Tradition says the famous frontier explorer Henry Weidner (Whitener), had persuaded young John to accompany him on an expedition into the wilderness of the upper Catawba flowing through the Blue Mountains.

They were impressed by the Pleasant Gardens area (near present-day Marion, in McDowell County, North Carolina), its rich soil and virgin forest abounding in game. It was common in pioneer days to have wrestling matches to establish a man's standing in a section or to settle friendly disputes. Henry Weidner had quite a reputation as a wrestler. Weidner and young John wrestled to decide which had the right to claim this beautiful spot.

John put forth a mighty effort, and flipped Weidner with a leg wrap, thereby winning the match. Evidently, then and there, he made up his mind to settle there. It was he who chose the name "Pleasant Gardens."

Hunting John's log cabin at Pleasant Gardens was burned by the Cherokees during the Cherokee uprising of 1776. Also lost were his books and accounts, while his plantation was ravaged. Pleasant Gardens, lying north of the Earl of Granville Line, was in Rowan County at that date. The southern tip of McDowell County, south of the Granville line, was in Old Tryon County, which later became the counties of Rutherford, Mecklenburg, McDowell, Buncombe, and Haywood.

Courtesy of The MacDowell News, *from July 28, 2008, article by Mike Conley*

Pleasant Gardens became a local historic landmark in 2008.

Round Hill, the old home site and family burial ground, can be easily seen from under the old mulberry trees in the yard of the McDowell House in Marion, McDowell County. The original log cabin home of Hunting John was against the hill directly across from the McDowell House.

The present house was built in the yard of the first home, the log cabin. Farther down the hill are the remains of an old brick kiln, where the bricks for the present house were probably made by McDowell slaves. Built in the late 1780s by Hunting John's son Joseph (of Pleasant Gardens), the house is of the Federal Period, when homes of wealthy families were more spacious, ornamental, and comfortable. Approaching the front doors, a filled-in door can be seen above, this being a one-time entrance from an upstairs porch, an architectural characteristic of river houses of that period.

On both ends of the house are the old freestanding chimneys. The fan lights above the two front doors are of the original old glass, Chinese Chippendale. Some panes of original glass remain in the end windows downstairs and in a number of those upstairs. Entering, one notices at once the original old fireplaces. These have been preserved both upstairs and downstairs. The double fireplaces on the right served to heat two rooms, the partitions having been removed in the present arrangement.

The original mantels have been lost. The wainscoting and hostess station are of the original old brick taken from the fireplace and chimney of the old dining room, now being used as a kitchen. The old hand-hewn beams, both upstairs and down, are just as they were many years ago. The uprights taken from the old house, damaged and worm-eaten but original, were saved and used. Unchanged are the upstairs floors; even the balcony railings are made from wood of the original house, treasured and reused whenever possible.

The early McDowells of Virginia and the Carolinas were planters and owned large plantations with slaves, growing corn and hemp in Virginia, and including corn and livestock in the Carolinas.

❋ ❋ ❋

The time was rapidly approaching when service to the King would no longer be tolerable. The Scots-Irish and other emigrants to America already enjoyed a far greater amount of autonomy from the Crown than the people of Great Britain and Ireland. British "push" was going to come to American "shove" over taxation, representation, and the colonists' burning desire for independence. The McDowells of Pennsylvania, Virginia, and the Carolinas were prominent Whigs, patriots, and commanders during the American Revolution. No family provided more sons and patriots for that cause than the McDowells.

They came to the Carolinas on the Great Wagon Road, and they helped to make great advances in many parts of the South. And, like the Scots-Irish throughout the continent, many of their descendants headed west to such promising locales as Tennessee, Missouri, and California to help complete the settling of North America.

Toward Revolution

Leo B. McDowell

After the English won the French and Indian War in 1763, the American colonists and especially the Scots-Irish were full of self-confidence and ready to take on anything. They started becoming active in the governance of the colonies and working toward autonomy and independence.

When the English proposed new taxes on the colonies to pay for reconstruction of the economy and military forces, the colonists objected strenuously. Many of the King's tax collectors were beaten, tarred and feathered, and ridden out of town on rails. When another tariff was imposed on many goods sent to the colonies—tea, for example—the colonists became fed up.

The Calvinists of New England fired the first shots in the Revolutionary War and were soon joined by the Scots-Irish from Pennsylvania, Maryland, Virginia, and the Carolinas. The Scots-Irish took control of Pennsylvania and Frederick County, Maryland, by establishing Revolutionary Committees.

The framework for independence was created in Philadelphia. John Hancock and Charles Thompson—both from Londonderry, Ireland—received a draft of the constitution. Five of the signers of the final document were Scots-Irish. The Scots-Irish of Pennsylvania, Maryland, and Virginia pledged themselves to the revolution. Justices in these colonies administered loyalty oaths to the cause of independence. Sympathizers to the Crown were severely dealt with, accordingly.

Samuel McDowell

Judge Samuel McDowell of Rockbridge County, Virginia, presided over one such case of the Commonwealth of Virginia against Alexander Miller:

> Upon considering the charges against Alexander Miller, the
> defendant, as well as the evidence adduced in support of the
> same, and also the verdict of the jury, we, the Court, are of
> opinion that the matter, as far as it relates to aiding and giving
> intelligence to the enemy, comes within the ordinance of
> Convention, and therefore give judgment: That the said Miller
> be confined to the bounds of the plantation whereon he now
> lives, in this County, till the end of the present war with Great
> Britain, and that he do not in any manner aid, abet,
> correspond, or converse with the enemies of America, nor

argue nor reason with any person or persons whatsoever on any political subject relating to the dispute between Britain and America, or until he be thence discharged by the Executive Power, or General Assembly, of the Commonwealth of Virginia; and in the meantime he, the said Miller, be kept in safe custody until he shall enter into bond himself in the sum of one hundred pounds and two good securities in the sum of fifty pounds each.

And that the whole of the costs of this prosecution be levied on the estate of said Alexander Miller. viz: To Thomas Smith and James Hill, they finding themselves and horses for going 120 miles to William Hutchison's, on Indian Creek, in Botetourt County, each at the rate of 4 pence per mile, and for returning the same distance with the prisoner, at the rate of 4 pence per mile each. To Robert McFarland, summoned by the officer; to assist, for going 50 miles, at 4 pence per mile.

To the witnesses for attending one day each, 25 pounds of tobacco, or two shillings and one penny, viz: William Ewing, Silas Hart, Mary Erwin, James Montgomery, William Givens, Robert McFarland, Thomas Smith, and James Hill. To the clerk, for attendance two days, twenty shillings. To the sheriff, for attending the Court and summoning the jury, twenty shillings. To Daniel Kidd, for summoning the witnesses, in which he rode 150 miles, at 4 pence per mile. And that the clerk issue executions for the above sums, respectively, when required thereto by the claimants.

~ Samuel McDowell

Judge Samuel McDowell, the son of Capt. John McDowell of Virginia, was a captain in the French and Indian War, commissioned on August 16, 1759. On November 21, 1759, he was installed as County Commissioner and justice in Rockbridge County, Virginia. In 1774, Samuel was a captain of the Rangers Company at the Battle of Point Pleasant, where he served as aide-de-camp to Gen. Isaac Shelby, who later became the first governor of Kentucky. Samuel became a colonel in the Revolutionary War, serving in Nathaniel Greene's campaign in North Carolina, and was with the army that drove General Cornwallis to Wilmington.

In 1775, in conjunction with his kinsman Thomas Lewis (son of settler John and brother of the hero of Point Pleasant), Samuel was chosen to represent the freeholders of Augusta in the convention at Richmond, Virginia. Samuel was also a member of the second convention that met at Williamsburg in 1776.

He served with his two eldest sons, John and James, as officers in the Revolutionary War; his youngest son, Samuel, was a private. He held the rank of colonel and distinguished himself in the battle of Guilford Court House. He raised a battalion at his own expense to aid in repelling the invasion of Virginia by Benedict Arnold. In 1783 he was appointed with Col. Thomas Marshall as a surveyor of the public lands in Fayette County, then one-third of Kentucky. Samuel, like his father and many of the other McDowells, was trained in the skills of surveying.

McDowells in the Revolutionary War

During the Revolutionary War, the McDowells of North Carolina, as members and commanders of the militias of "Overmountain" and "Backwater" men, fought victoriously in numerous battles. McDowell County in western North Carolina is named in honor of Col. Joseph "Pleasant Gardens" McDowell, who distinguished himself during the war by employing guerrilla warfare against numerically superior Loyalist forces. His cousins, Brig. Gen. Charles McDowell (born 1743, married Grace "Grizzel" Greenlee Bowman in 1760) and Maj. Joseph "Quaker Meadows" McDowell (born 1756) also served in the war.

Much of the activity involving the McDowells and other Scots-Irish took place after Gen. Lord Charles Cornwallis, the British commander, appointed Maj. Patrick Ferguson as inspector of militia for South Carolina to defeat the local militia and recruit Loyalists. Ferguson's opposition included men from South Carolina's backwoods under Thomas "the Gamecock" Sumter including William McDowell, North Carolinians commanded by Gen. Charles McDowell (the son of Joseph McDowell, born 1715), and Overmountain men from today's Tennessee under Gen. Isaac Shelby, who later became the first governor of Kentucky and the father-in-law of Dr. Ephraim McDowell[*].

Moving into North Carolina, Ferguson attempted to intimidate the western settlers, threatening to march into the mountains and "lay waste the country with fire and sword" if they did not lay down their arms and pledge allegiance to the King.

On September 2, 1780, Ferguson, with about 70 American Loyalist Volunteers and several hundred Tory militiamen, set out for western North Carolina and the foothills of the Blue Ridge Mountains. Lt. Anthony Allaire maintained his diary of marches and "getting in motion," providing a graphic report of what kind of medical attention awaited the wounded in the back country.

---

[*] Born 1771, a son of Col. Samuel McDowell (born 1735) of Virginia and later of Kentucky. See "Samuel (John and Magdalene's Son)," page 69.

At Wofford's iron works, they met a "Rebel militia-man that got wounded in the right arm at the skirmish at Cedar Springs, the 8th of August. The bone was very much shattered. It was taken off by one (Mr.) Frost, a blacksmith, with a shoemaker's knife and carpenter's saw. He stopped the blood with the fungus of the oak, without taking up a blood vessel." We can only assume that the Rebel's anesthetic was a liberal supply of whiskey. But given the state of surgery then and the resemblance of military field hospitals to slaughterhouses, the Rebel could have been in worse hands than Frost the blacksmith.

On September 7, Ferguson and his men crossed into North Carolina and marched to Gilbert Town (later Rutherfordton), about 55 miles west of Charlotte, where Ferguson set up his base of operations. Allaire described it as containing "one dwelling house, one barn, a blacksmith's shop, and some out-houses."

Allaire described a skirmish with Col. Charles McDowell's band on Cane Creek, about 21 miles north of Gilbert Town, where 40 American Loyalist Volunteers and 100 Tory militia came into contact with the Rebels: "We totally routed...those congress heroes. Our loss was two wounded and one killed." Rebel accounts collected years after the skirmish claimed that McDowell initiated the action and that several Tories were killed before the Rebels retreated.

Charles McDowell and his men crossed the mountains and took refuge with the Overmountain Men at the Watauga Settlements. Two days later, Allaire wrote that "the poor, deluded people of this Province begin to be sensible of their error, and come in very fast."

Both Allaire and Patrick Ferguson were unaware that Col. Charles McDowell had concocted a plan, coming into play. Many of the people coming in to take British protection and even to swear oaths of allegiance to George III were doing so as part of McDowell's deliberate Rebel policy to save the region's cattle herds.

According to statements in 1797 by two prominent North Carolina militia officers who participated in the campaign, Maj. Joseph McDowell and Col. David Vance, Colonel McDowell suggested this trick to the leading men of the country. Some refused and drove all the cattle they could find to the heads of deep mountain glens. "Hunting" John McDowell had driven his cattle up to the cove. But others were prevailed upon to follow Charles McDowell's suggestion. In doing so, they risked the brunt of public criticism for their actions, because this policy to deceive the British and save Rebel herds could not be shared with the populace lest leaks occur.

Patrick Ferguson eventually suspected the ruse. His men were in need of meat, and he took a force into the field to search for Rebel cattle. Accompanying him was the noted Indian fighter, Capt.—later Colonel—

John Carson, who was one of the men who had agreed to Col. Charles' plan. John Carson was the husband of Rachel Matilda McDowell and later of Mary Moffett McDowell, the widow of Col. Joseph "Pleasant Gardens" McDowell. Both women were close relatives of Col. Charles McDowell, the Patriot commander.

Ferguson found a large herd roaming in the cane-breaks. His men assumed that the cattle belonged to Rebels and began slaughtering them. John Carson knew who owned the cattle, and watched without comment until over 100 head had been slaughtered. Then he observed that the cattle may have belonged to Tories who had joined Ferguson's force. The upshot of this incident was that the owners of the cattle, loyal Tories all, were incensed, and the Rebels made sure that the story was spread abroad. Patrick Ferguson realized he had been outwitted.

John Carson's good name, temporarily sacrificed for the Rebel cause, was not easily recovered. Many years after the Revolution a man charged that John Carson had been a Tory. John Carson's son, Samuel Price Carson, a member of Congress, thereupon challenged the slanderer to a duel and killed him.

Allaire realized that the countryside harbored people not "sensible of their error." On September 15, with 40 American Volunteers and a few hundred militia, he "got in motion" again. He found a four-mile stretch of Cane Creek "so amazingly crooked that we were obliged to cross it nineteen times," and on the following day encountered a "very handsome place," still known as Pleasant Gardens (the home of Hunting John McDowell's family), a settlement "composed of the most violent Rebels I ever saw, particularly the young ladies."

The hospitality was just as thin at Quaker Meadows. Prior to the Battle of Kings Mountain on October 7, where Col. Joseph of Pleasant Gardens, Col. Charles, and his brother Maj. Joseph McDowell were leading figures, men from Colonel Ferguson's army visited Quaker Meadows and ransacked the McDowells' house, appropriating the clothing of Charles and Joseph. They told the men's mother, Margaret O'Neill McDowell, who presided over the house, that when they caught Charles they would kill him outright. They said they would kill Joe on bended knees after humiliating him by making him beg for his life. The Irish Margaret, far from being intimidated, told them to be careful lest the British do all the begging.

Margaret, by her defiance of the Tories, is one of the few women recognized by the Daughters of the Revolution as a patriot of the Revolution. A striking woman, intelligent, articulate, and with a tendency to speak her mind born of a deep-rooted hatred of the English, Margaret was a daughter of Laird Samuel O'Neill of County Antrim. She was born and raised in Ireland's Shane's Castle, the home of the O'Neills and descendants of the great Con O'Neill and Hugh O'Neill—the leader of Tyrone's Rebellion.

In response to the British invasion, a furious army formed on the western frontier. Growing in numbers as they marched east, some 900 men gave chase to Ferguson, surrounding his army at Kings Mountain, South Carolina, and killing or capturing Ferguson's entire command.

Pieces from Colonel Ferguson's china dinnerware were presented to Col. Joseph McDowell of Pleasant Gardens (born 1758) in recognition of his heroism at Kings Mountain and are still prized by family members. Thomas Jefferson referred to this victory as "That Turn of the Tide of Success."

Ferguson's defeat was a stunning blow to British fortunes. The strength of the Patriot militia was affirmed. The hoped-for Loyalist support didn't materialize. Cornwallis was forced to pull back from North Carolina, giving the Continental Army time to bring fresh regulars and new commanders south. On January 17, 1781, Daniel Morgan, using Continentals and militia, under Maj. John McDowell (another son of Capt. Joseph McDowell of North Carolina), defeated Col. Banastre Tarleton's British army at Cowpens, South Carolina.

What followed was a winter campaign between Cornwallis and the armies of Morgan and Nathanael Greene. Try as Cornwallis might, the Americans always seemed to cross the river to safety before Cornwallis could cut them off.

At Guilford Courthouse, North Carolina, on March 15, Greene finally turned to face Cornwallis. Greene's army, including the militia of Col. Samuel McDowell, was driven from the battlefield, but Cornwallis suffered severe losses which he could not replace. Greene's army included the Rockbridge Militia, commanded by Col. Samuel McDowell (born 1735), who in June of 1781, was sworn in at Staunton, Virginia, as a member of the Governor's Council alongside Governor Nelson.

Cornwallis pulled back to recuperate, moving his army north into Virginia without subduing North Carolina. In the fall of 1781, George Washington rushed his army south to join French reinforcements. When French warships gained control of Chesapeake Bay, Cornwallis was besieged and forced to surrender on October 19, 1781, just over a year after Kings Mountain.

Grace McDowell

The story of Grace "Grizzel" Greenlee Bowman McDowell, like her gravestone in Quaker Meadows cemetery, is time-worn and seldom contemplated. The short pamphlet biography written by William Carson Ervin (a cousin to the McDowells through both the Erwins and Carsons) was published by the North Carolina Society of the Daughters of the

American Revolution at the turn of the century. It is out of print and, in intervening years, has acquired some of the flavor of an old-fashioned Valentine. Though her story is Early American, there are elements redolent of the Old World.

She was christened with a melodious name, but was also known as Grizzel (Grissel or Grizel), an old French variant of the name Grace, held in the McDowell (MacDowall) family since their days in Scotland. It is a name most applicable to a pretty girl or, at least, one endowed with the indefinable quality of charm. Grizzel has a fairytale ring to it, but certain legends indicate that she had qualities that were also attributed to a later fictitious heroine called Katie "Scarlett" O'Hara in *Gone With the Wind*.

Grace's mother, Mary Elizabeth McDowell Greenlee, lived to the age of 104, a circumstance (among others) that caused whispers to pass that her longevity was due to the practice of witchcraft.

Grace was born in a log cabin in the Shenandoah Valley of Virginia, settled by her parents' two families in 1737. Grace was only five years old when the French and Indian War erupted. During its long course, many people who were neighbors abandoned their cabin homes and forsook the valley, while others like the Greenlees and the McDowells stayed on and suffered the loss of family members and friends. Capt. John McDowell, one of her uncles, was killed in 1742 at the Battle of Balcony Falls.

The time eventually came when her father, James Greenlee, promised her in marriage to a wealthy landowner much older than she. It is obvious that Grace must have assented to this old world custom, though perhaps reluctantly.

In describing her first wedding day, her biographer said "that the wedding trousseau was prepared, the wedding feast in readiness, and that the ceremony had actually progressed to the point where the bride-to-be was asked if she would take the ancient bridegroom for 'better or for worse,' when she electrified the guests by a most emphatic 'No!'"

But another wedding day came when Grace was not a reluctant bride, and she married John Bowman, the young man of her choice. After moving to North Carolina with her husband, he was mortally wounded at the Battle of Ramsour's Mill. Upon hearing of his wounding, Grace rode to him on horseback, carrying her little daughter Mary "Polly." She followed "dim trails through the South Mountains," reaching her husband a short time before he died. She buried her husband near where he fell and, in deep grief, rode home again with little Polly a comforting burden in her arms. She may have written the following eulogy, attributed to her when it was found "among Bowman papers" later:

Like the rising sun in the morn
He went away, left me forlorn
And saw the tears I shed;
My boding heart did then foretell
That fated evening heard the knell
That my dear John had bled.
Tears that must ever fall!
For ah no lights the past recall,
No cries awoke the dead.
Weep not Polly for I will be
A mother and father unto thee oh.

She became a planter, and from the fruit of her fields and the fields of others became a procurer of supplies for the rebel Whigs and their unofficial quartermaster, with wagons of food and supplies going for their need. She had encounters with local Tories and sometimes bested them. Her biographer records:

> On one occasion...she pursued some Tories who had
> plundered her home...and compelled the robbers, at the point
> of a musket, to give up her property...another story…is that on
> one occasion some of Tarleton's troopers carried away some
> of the Bowman horses. This courageous woman rode into the
> British camp some miles away and demanded her horses from
> the officer in charge, and was allowed to bring them back in
> triumph. In 1782 she married her cousin, Charles McDowell,
> and went to live at McDowell Station (Quaker Meadows) and
> shared the house with Margaret O'Neill McDowell, her
> mother-in-law.

Grace bore five McDowell children:

> Senators, judges, soldiers, lawyers, leaders in business and the
> professions are her sons. Brilliant and beautiful women are her
> daughters.

Grace was only 32 when she married Charles McDowell. It was written of her:

> Though it cannot be said with any certainty that she lived
> happily ever after, the wilderness girl, after the end of the
> second war she had experienced, their nearness to her almost
> participation, became, for her time and area, the Great Lady,
> and we hope that she had some silken dresses for her back, for
> her new husband (Charles), we know, after he no longer wore
> his uniform, did, on occasion, wear velvet knee britches with
> silver buckles at the knee, and silver buckles on his shoes."

Other McDowell Patriots

Many other McDowells served during the American Revolution including Maj. John McDowell (born in 1757 in Virginia and married to Hannah Keller, the daughter of Hannah McDowell and John Keller), Maj. James McDowell of Mecklenburg County (commander at the Battle of Cowpens), Col. John McDowell of Mecklenburg County, William McDowell of South Carolina, Ensign James McDowell, Lt. John McDowell, and two doctors named John McDowell.

Skirmishes in North Carolina were commonplace between the supporters of Independence and Loyalist Tories. A noted Tory was killed by James Gray on Col. John McDowell's plantation (Cleghorn) in Mecklenburg County prior to the gathering for the impending battle at Kings Mountain. From Scotland to Ulster to Rutherford County, the Scots-Irish had survived centuries of living in a hard environment, which made them hard, both physically and socially.

Many of the area's Scots-Irish—mostly Presbyterians—came together at Sycamore Shoals. The force included Col. William Campbell (kin to the McDowells of Virginia) and his men from western Virginia, Isaac Shelby, and John Sevier. They agreed to pursue Ferguson, but first paused for a religious service. After all, six of the commanders were elders of the church: Colonels Campbell, Cleveland, (Charles) McDowell, Shelby, Sevier, and Williams.

It was fitting that they would worship along with their womenfolk and children, under the preaching of the Reverend Sam Doaks, a Presbyterian minister. He had done his share of fighting but did not go after Ferguson with them, instead staying in defense of the women and children.

He preached a powerful sermon admonishing the men to do their duty in the upcoming battle. He prayed to the Lord, noting the similarities of these men to the army of Gideon in the fight against the Midianites. He ended his prayer with the words of Gideon when he instructed his men to surround the enemy and on the signal of the trumpets to shout, "The Sword of the Lord and of Gideon."

The minister paused, then raised his arms and his voice to the gathering and told them, "Let that be your battle cry. The Sword of the Lord and of Gideon." The men shouted back, "The Sword of the Lord and of Gideon."

As a general in the Revolutionary War, **Charles McDowell**, the son of Capt. Joseph McDowell (born 1715) of Virginia and North Carolina, commanded a regiment of 160 soldiers from Burke and Rutherford counties in North Carolina. His troops fought at the battle of Kings Mountain, although he was not present during the battle. He served as the commander of forces that captured and destroyed a fort in June 1780 at the Pacolet River. Brig. Gen. Charles McDowell commanded with Gen. Isaac Shelby at Cedar Hill, and commanded forces at Musgrove Hill and Cave Creek. On September 12, 1780, Gen. Charles McDowell ambushed part of Ferguson's army at Cane Creek but was driven off, and fled to Sycamore Shoals to await reinforcement by the Overmountain men.

In late September 1780, William and his cousin Arthur Campbell assembled the Washington County, Virginia, militia. Isaac Shelby, John Sevier, and William Campbell mustered the militia of the Watauga and Holston Valleys at Sycamore Shoals of the Watauga River (Elizabethton) to join the Burke County militia under Charles McDowell. Fort Watauga is today reconstructed at the Tennessee historic area. This was North Carolina in 1780, the State of Franklin (or Frankland) later, and the Southwest Territory later on.

On September 30, 1780, North Carolinians under Benjamin Cleveland, Joseph Winston, and William Lenoir joined the Overmountain men at the McDowell home at Quaker Meadows. On October 1 and 2, 1780, the army stopped and camped to dry out, preparing for battle.

It was time, Charles McDowell decided, to hand over his command to a regular Continental Army officer, and the post went to the capable Gen. William Campbell of Virginia. Campbell's descendants were cousins to the Prestons and McDowells of Virginia. General McDowell thereupon resigned his commission, but continued to support the patriots by manufacturing powder with the help of his wife, Grace Grizzel Greenlee Bowman McDowell, and secretly carrying it to the army for use at the Battle of Kings Mountain on October 7, 1780.

Charles later served as a member of the North Carolina State Senate in 1782–1788 and of the North Carolina House of Commons in 1809–1810.

His brother, **Maj. Joseph "Quaker Meadows" McDowell**, entered the army in General Charles' regiment in February 1776, at the age of 22. He fought in expeditions against the Scots Tories and the Cherokee Indians, who had attacked the Catawba settlements. In July 1776 he, his brother Charles, and nine other men helped defend a fort containing 120 women and children against the Cherokees.

They were also on the Rutherford campaign against the Cherokees. Their other battles included Ramsour's Mill, Musgrave's Mill, Earle's Ford on the Pacolet, the Cowpens in January 1781, and Kings Mountain in October 1780, where his cousin Colonel Joseph of Pleasant Gardens was in charge of the regiment. A history by Draper noted: "The bayonet charge down the mountain by Ferguson's regulars was driven back by the well directed fire from the rifles of [Gen. Isaac] Shelby's and [Col. Joseph] McDowell's men. The victory was complete."

This is the source of a long-running dispute within the family. Descendants of both Josephs (of Quaker Meadows and Pleasant Gardens) claim their respective Joseph was the hero of Kings Mountain. The combined evidence indicates that Col. Joseph of Pleasant Gardens was indeed the Joseph McDowell to be credited here. The monument at Kings Mountain bears the name of neither—testament to the strength of the contentions of both sides.

As an aftermath of the Battle of Kings Mountain, 36 Tories were tried for treason and sentenced to be hanged. Among the group that was tried by the ad hoc military council were the brothers John and Arthur McFall. John McFall almost was acquitted. All he had done was verbally abuse a Rebel's wife and whip their 10-year old son with a switch cut from a tree—the boy refused to feed the horses of McFall's band and told McFall, "If you want your horses fed, feed them yourself."

Maj. Joseph McDowell recommended leniency. Col. Benjamin Cleveland disagreed: "That man, McFall, went to the house of Martin Davenport, one of my best soldiers, when he was away from home fighting for his country, insulted his wife, and whipped his child, and no such man ought to be allowed to live." McFall was found guilty.

The McDowells were successful in saving John McFall's brother, Arthur, who after the war became a famous hunter in the mountains and never forgot the McDowells for saving him. He lived to between the ages of 90 and 100. Of the 36 convicted, only nine were actually hanged. One of the men who received mercy that day told Col. Isaac Shelby, who had proposed after the first nine that the hangings should end, "You have saved my life, and I will tell you a secret. (Gen. Banastre) Tarleton will be here in the morning. A woman has brought the news."

General Tarleton was known as Bloody Tarleton or Bloody Ban since his butchery at the Battle of Waxhaws. "Tarleton's Quarter" became synonymous with "No Prisoners."

In 1779 Maj. Joseph "Quaker Meadows" McDowell fought in the Stono expedition. In the Revolutionary forces, while serving under his brother, Charles, the commander of District, he fought in all the battles of western North Carolina.

Entering the service of the state at the close of the war, he was sent to the House of Commons in 1787, serving until 1792. In 1788 he was a delegate to the North Carolina Constitutional Convention, in which he was a leader of the opposition that rejected the Federal Constitution until a Bill of Rights was added.

He entered the U.S. Congress in 1797, where for seven years he was an active opponent of the Federalists. He served in 1787 as a commissioner for settling the boundary line between Tennessee and North

Carolina. He was influential as a Republican (Whig) leader in the western section of his state of North Carolina.

Maj. John McDowell, son of Col. Samuel McDowell of Virginia and Kentucky, served as the commander of Company 1 of Morgan's Rifle Regiment, commanded by Gen. Daniel Morgan at the Battle of Saratoga.

Morgan's Regiment was recruited from the settlers of Pennsylvania, Maryland, and Virginia. They often were the first in the field and last out. A report to Congress accorded the glory of the action at the Battle of Saratoga, New York, in September and October, 1777, "entirely to the valor of the rifle regiment and corps of light infantry under the command of Col. Morgan." Each of Morgan's men was armed with a rifle, tomahawk, and long knife, and they were known as "The Corps of Rangers."

They dressed in flannel shirts, cloth or buckskin breeches, buckskin leggings, and moccasins. On top, they wore brown linen or buckskin hunting shirts confined by a belt holding the knife and tomahawk. They wore caps on which appeared the words, "Liberty or Death." Morgan's Regiment was "the corps the army of Gen. Burgoyne was most afraid of." John McDowell also served with General George Washington at the crossing of the Delaware, at the battles of Princeton and Trenton, and at Valley Forge, Pennsylvania, where they starved and suffered during the cold winter.

He was wounded at Brandywine, and fought at the battles of Monmouth and Yorktown. Maj. John McDowell was awarded land grants in Kentucky in 1789 for his military service. He attained his rank of major during the War of 1812.

Sgt. John McDowell of South Carolina served with Lt. Col. Francis Marion, "the Swamp Fox," in the 2nd South Carolina Regiment Grenadier Company during the Revolutionary War from November 4, 1775 to November 1, 1779. He fought at the Battles of Sullivan's Island and Spring Hill Redoubt.

Not long after the war, **Col. (Judge) Samuel McDowell** of Virginia moved his family to Fayette County, Kentucky, and later to Harrodsburg. He received nearly 12,000 acres in land grants as a result of his war service. He was accompanied by his wife, Mary McClung McDowell, and nine of their children. Two of his daughters remained in Virginia.

He served on the bench until shortly before his death at the Kentucky home of his son, Joseph. He had been a member of the Virginia House of Burgesses in 1773. Samuel was appointed to the first District Court ever held in Kentucky in 1783 and was president of the convention called to frame the constitution for the state of Kentucky. As a judge in the 1st District Court in Kentucky, McDowell presided over nine conventions including the Constitutional Convention of Kentucky. Samuel sent a copy of the new constitution two weeks before its framing to President George Washington and received this reply:

> (To) Col. Samuel McDowell, Kentucky
> (From) Philadelphia
> 20 October 1792
>
> Sir,
>
> Your letter of the 6th of April, enclosing a copy of the
> Constitution formed for the State of Kentucky, did not get to
> my hands 'till I was about leaving this place to go to Mount
> Vernon, and I embrace the earliest opportunity, after my return
> to the seat of Government to acknowledge the receipt of it,
> and to thank you for the transmission.
>
> I am, Sir, with esteem,
> (President) Geo. Washington

At the age of 81, Colonel Samuel rode on horseback from Danville to Nashville to represent the church presbytery in a synodical convention, traveling an average of 40 miles per day.

As a matter of family loyalty, Samuel opened his household to his nephew, James McDowell, at age 16, after the death of Samuel's brother and James' father, Capt. James McDowell. James became a surveyor in Kentucky with his cousin Thomas Lewis, and helped to lay out the township of Danville, Kentucky.

Judge Samuel McDowell also organized the Danville Political Club, which shaped the future of the young State of Kentucky. He died in 1817 at the age of 84.

MacDowalls in the U.S. Civil War

William L. MacDougall and Leo B. McDowell

The name MacDowell figured prominently in the U.S. Civil War, from 1861 to 1865.

General Irvin McDowell

Leslie's Weekly

In the first major battle of the war, at Bull Run Creek near Manassas, Virginia, not far from the U.S. capital, Washington, D.C., the leading Northern general on the scene was Irvin McDowell. Born in Cincinnati, Ohio, in 1818, he was a descendant of the widely acclaimed Ephraim McDowell, one of the first of the name to arrive in America, in 1735. He was educated in France and later at the United States Military Academy at West Point from which he was graduated in 1838. He served competently in the Mexican War, but after that was mainly in staff jobs, not combat. Then, Irvin McDowell, who became a major general in the Union Army, had the bad luck to be named commander of the U.S. forces who rushed to meet the much better trained Confederate Army in the war's opening hours.

At the start of the Civil War in 1861, he was abruptly promoted from major to brigadier general and thrown into the first battle of the war, at Manassas, Virginia. McDowell's troops, whose movements were known in advance through the efforts of Confederate spies in Washington, were soundly defeated at Manassas. General McDowell was also present, in a lesser role, at the second Battle of Manassas a year later, also a humiliating defeat for the Yankees.

Despite being charged with malfeasance, McDowell was not at the end of his career, for he was cleared and promoted. He was widely admired by many of his colleagues, and was placed in command of U.S. forces on the Pacific Coast. He died in San Francisco in 1885.

A contemporary commentator concluded that McDowell

> was one of the best military scholars of the army and one of
> the most unsuccessful of its officers…His place in the sure
> judgment of coming times is secure. He will not be reckoned
> brilliant or great, but his abilities and devotion will be
> recognized. His manifold misfortunes, the amiability with

which he encountered personal reverses, the fortitude with which he endured calumny will be recounted. Men will do justice to the services he rendered us in our darkest hours, and he will leave an enduring and honorable fame.

Battle of McDowell

Another major battle in the early months of the war was fought, curiously enough, near the village of McDowell, Virginia, not far from the border of West Virginia. The Battle of McDowell occurred May 8 and 9, 1862, and is often regarded as the start of a successful sweep up the Shenandoah Valley that made the reputation of Confederate Maj. Gen. Thomas J. "Stonewall" Jackson, one of the South's most acclaimed military heroes.

Tiny McDowell, Virginia, named for an early Virginia governor, James McDowell, would seem an unlikely location for such a large battle. Like many similar villages up and down the valley settled a century before, it nestles between ridges of the Appalachian chain of mountains and was then reached with considerable difficulty over a few narrow and tortuous roads.

The fate of the war was in considerable doubt when Northern and Southern forces converged on McDowell in early 1862. The Union was winning battles in the American West, and despite the Confederate victory at Manassas, Jackson had already lost a battle in the Shenandoah Valley.

Suzanne O. McDougal

So it was with considerable concern that Jackson lined up his troops in the mountains overlooking McDowell and prepared for battle. At first, the Union forces marched without much opposition up steep Sitlington Hill and other nearby ridges. As they neared the top, Jackson opened fire on the Federals, and they fell back—but not without inflicting heavy casualties on the Confederates.

The Battle of McDowell was considered a pyrrhic victory for the South, which suffered 498 casualties compared with 256 for the Yankees. But it was enough to reverse the fortunes of the Confederacy for a considerable time afterward.

The Highland Historical Society concludes that the "engagement west of Staunton, Virginia, in the mountains of Highland County, in the tiny village of McDowell, turned the tide of the Civil War in the theater of Virginia."

Today's residents of the area are proud that, unlike some other Civil War battle sites, McDowell and its vicinity have not changed significantly. A museum in the village featuring many aspects of the battle welcomes visitors, and reenactments present a first-hand view of the fighting.

Suzanne O. McDougal

**This church in McDowell served as
hospital for both Blue and Gray**

James Charles Sheffield McDowell

Many MacDowells of various ages and backgrounds were active in the war—emulating their fighting ancestors over the centuries.

One eminent officer was Col. James Charles Sheffield McDowell, of Quaker Meadows, Burke County, North Carolina. He was a colonel in the Confederate Army as part of "Stonewall" Jackson's 2nd Corps, 54th Infantry Regiment of North Carolina.

At the Battle of Chancellorsville, Virginia, which some consider the Confederacy's greatest victory, Colonel McDowell commanded the 1st North Carolina Regiment in Colston's 3rd Brigade. He was one of 26 officers mortally wounded defending Marye's Heights, May 4, 1863.

He was the last male heir of Capt. Charles McDowell, builder of McDowell House at Quaker Meadows.

His body, along with the body of Gen. Stonewall Jackson (also killed at Chancellorsville), was taken to the Confederate capitol in Richmond, Virginia, where they lay in state, side by side. McDowell's body was then moved to Raleigh, North Carolina, where he is buried in the New Bern Cemetery.

William Wallace McDowell

Another prominent Carolinian was Capt. William Wallace McDowell of the Pleasant Gardens McDowells. He was elected captain of the Buncombe Riflemen of the Town of Asheville, which wore uniforms that were the envy of many in the South. They were described as consisting of "steel mixed cassimere," and trimmed in green velvet, with a row of gilt buttons on the breast, three buttons on the wristbands, and six on the skirts. The gray trousers bore a green worsted stripe down each leg. The captain's uniform was identical, except that it was additionally trimmed in gold lace.

The company colors were a blue flag with a white diamond in the center. On it in red were the arms of the State and under them a scroll with the word, "Ready." The riflemen drilled once a month, more often "when necessary."

A flag made for the volunteers by the ladies of Asheville was adopted as the regimental flag by the 1st North Carolina Infantry Regiment, commanded by Gen. D. H. Hill.

When news of the opening battle of the war at Fort Sumter, South Carolina, reached North Carolina, Governor John W. Ellis wasted no time in preparing the state for war. In response to the U.S. Secretary of War's request for two regiments for the Union Army, Ellis replied: "You can get no troops from North Carolina."

On April 18, 1861, the Buncombe Riflemen, preparing to march to the railroad at Morganton, lined up on a street in the courthouse square. Much of the town turned out for the farewell, and McDowell's cousins, Anna and Lillie Woodfin, presented the company with a flag of red, white, and blue silk made from their own dresses. Anna Woodfin, who made the presentation speech, embroidered the word "BETHEL" onto the flag after the war.

Captain McDowell's courage at the Big Bethel Church Battle on June 1, 1861, was commended by General Hill and others. He was promoted to major in the 60th North Carolina Infantry Regiment, in which his brother, Joseph, served as colonel.

Described as a tall, well-built, bearded man of quiet, courtly manner, William McDowell was renowned for his fairness, integrity, loyalty, and courage. He is buried at Riverside Cemetery in Asheville.

Alexander McDowell McCook

On the other side in the war, Alexander McDowell McCook, born in Ohio in 1831, played a prominent role for the Union. An 1852 graduate of West Point, McCook was considered a brilliant tactician and served as professor at the military academy when the Civil War broke out. He rose rapidly to major general after combat service at the First Battle of Manassas, the capture of Nashville, the Battle of Shiloh, and the advance on Chattanooga.

At the Battle of Chickamauga, he and his force were caught up in the general retreat of the Federals, and his reputation suffered even though he was cleared of any wrongdoing.

He retired as a major general after serving as a staff officer for Gen. William T. Sherman. He died in 1903.

William Hugh McDowell

One of the most acclaimed heroes of the war was Cadet Pvt. William "Willie" Hugh McDowell, born December 31, 1846. He was the son of Robert Irwin McDowell, a prominent businessman and treasurer of Davidson College of Charlotte, North Carolina.

Cadet McDowell entered the Virginia Military Institute in 1863 with a letter of recommendation from his cousin, Mary Anna Morrison Jackson, the wife of Gen. Thomas Stonewall Jackson.

Virginia Military Institute Archives

As the war neared its end, the Confederacy found it harder and harder to keep its ranks filled, and the cadet corps of Virginia Military Institute stepped up to take its place on the battle lines at New Market, Virginia. Some 247 of the cadets moved to the front line in their splendid uniforms—at first jeered by the weary and dirty Confederate veterans—but they soon won the respect of virtually everybody.

They fought valiantly, but they were overwhelmed by the advancing Yankees. More than 50 of the cadets fell dead or wounded, including McDowell.

An observer wrote: "In advancing from the ravine the [VMI] Battalion was now and then protected by folds in the ground from the direct fire of the enemy. From the ravine to the close of the Bushong House is about half a mile. The cadets were exposed to direct fire the last half of this distance, losing three killed at this stage of their advance, the number including First Sergeant Cabell of D Co., and Privates Stanard and McDowell of B Co."

Another wrote: "A little removed from the spot where (First Sergeant) Cabell fell, and nearer to the position of the enemy, lay (Pvt.) McDowell, it was a sight to wring one's heart. That little boy was lying there asleep, more fit, indeed, for the cradle than the grave."

William L. MacDougall

Path in New Market where Willie McDowell fell

The author noted that the young man "had torn open his jacket and shirt, and, even in death, lay clutching them back, exposing a fair breast with its red wound."

McDowell is referred to as "the Ghost of VMI" and is buried beneath the "Virginia Mourns" monument at the campus of VMI in Lexington, Virginia.

He was 17 years old.

Thain MacDowell: Hero

Scott A. MacDougald

When Thain Wendell MacDowell was born in his great grandmother's house—the parsonage of the village of Lachute, Quebec, Canada—on September 16, 1890, there surely was no indication that by the age of 26 this son of a Methodist minister would become one of his country's greatest war heroes.

A year after he was born, his father moved the family to Lyn, Ontario. His father died in 1894, then Thain's mother remarried and moved Thain and his siblings (brothers Cyler, Newell, Merrill and sister Eula), to the village of Maitland, Ontario, in 1897. Thain's new stepfather was the local cheese maker and is credited for being an exemplary father to his readymade family.

Star Weekly, June 14, 1919

Thain attended Maitland Public School, and graduated from the Brockville Collegiate Institute before attending the University of Toronto, where he excelled in sports and academics. He graduated with a bachelor of arts degree in 1914.

World War I began in August 1914. Thain volunteered for the army and was appointed as a Provisional Lieutenant with the 41st Regiment (Brockville Rifles) on November 9, 1914. On January 9, 1915, he enlisted for overseas service as a Lieutenant in the 38th (Ottawa) Battalion, Canadian Expeditionary Force. After training in London, Ontario; Bermuda; and then England, he arrived in France on August 3, 1916. His battalion was sent to fight in the trench warfare of northern France as part of the 4th Canadian Division. It was while fighting with the Allied forces in the Battle of the Somme that Thain would win the Distinguished Service Order for his gallantry.

Battle of the Somme

The Battle of the Somme began with costly Allied attacks on German lines on July 1, 1916, which lasted until November 28. The terrain was horrible to cross, the firing was murderous, and the Allied artillery shells did not destroy enough of the belts of barb wire set up as barriers to impede Allied infantry attacks across No Man's Land. In these five months the Allied line moved forward only six miles at a terrible cost in human life. The Allies had suffered about 650,000 casualties, the Germans suffered about 500,000 casualties, including about 200,000 deaths on each side. The Somme cost Canada 24,029 casualties as the Canadian soldiers confirmed their reputation as hard-hitting shock troops; for the remainder of the war they were brought in to lead the assault in one battle after another.

The conditions on the Somme were truly awful. Mud in the trenches was often up to the hips and it was not an uncommon sight to find men stuck in the mud and having to be dug out. The weather was very bad. When the newly arrived 4th Division took its place in the line it faced an almost unbelievable ordeal of knee-deep mud and tenacious enemy resistance. Despite the curtain of fire, on November 11 the 4th Division captured the long-sought Regina Trench, only to find it reduced to a mere depression in the chalk by the many thousands of explosive artillery shells.

The next objective in the German line was Desire Trench, which ran east and west across the Miraumont roads, 200 meters north of what is now the Adanac cemetery. On November 18, 1916, in the final Allied attack of the Battle of the Somme, they advanced northward to capture Desire Trench in a driving snowstorm.

At Desire Trench the newly promoted Capt. Thain MacDowell won the Distinguished Service Order medal for his heroism. His sister Eula's grandson, Charles Dumbrille, wrote a biography of Thain that describes what happened:

> Here, as Captain of "B" Company, he led his battalion against
> the German trenches in an attack south of Ancre against
> Desire Trench and Desire Support Trench on November 18,
> 1916. Bravely, MacDowell advanced to within throwing
> distance of the enemy and bombed out three German machine
> gun nests which had been holding up the advance. He then
> was able to capture, after brutal hand to hand combat, three
> Officers and 50 of the enemy and clear the way for his
> battalion to advance to the final objective.

Vimy Ridge

As a result of being wounded in this action, he was invalided back to England, but returned to France by January 1917 to rejoin the 4th Division at Vimy Ridge. In 1917 he was promoted to Major. For the first time, all the Canadian units were being brought together to fight as one united army. The objective was the now famous Vimy Ridge.

After the fighting of the Somme, the German Army had withdrawn its bulging front line on a 100-mile stretch of the Western Front to the heavily fortified Hindenburg Line. Vimy Ridge was a very strong German position on a key height of land and strategic to the new German defensive line. Its high ground dominated the Douai Plain of northern France and looked out over Lens to the east and Arras to the south. With its view of a great stretch of German-held territory, Vimy Ridge dominated the flatlands around it and was regarded as the backbone of the whole German position in France. Vimy Ridge had been assaulted without success by the French in 1915 and the British in 1916. When the Canadians arrived at Vimy, Allied efforts to seize the ridge at Vimy had already cost 300,000 casualties.

The vicious fighting had torn up the ground of No Man's Land with shellfire. Sappers had sunk many mine shafts, planted explosives underneath enemy positions, and cratered the landscape. The soggy, muddy battlefield was scarred by trenches and dugouts carved ever deeper over the years.

The German Sixth Army had an excellent view of the terrain and had had ample time to develop its defenses with three main defensive lines of trenches and deep dugouts protected by belts of barbed wire and concrete machine gun posts. The chalky soil of the ridge had been carved up with tunnels and communication trenches, and the supporting German second line located one to two miles farther east of the ridge featured vast underground bunkers, some of which could hold a battalion in safety.

The Canadian plan of attack relied on good reconnaissance and intensive planning. New tactics and methods were used. Maps, photographs and information were distributed down to platoon level, instead of just to officers as had been done in past Allied attacks. Platoons were equipped and trained to be self-sufficient fighting units, each with their own specific objectives for which they had trained intensively. Every soldier was familiarized with the objectives they sought and they repeatedly practiced each man's role for their own platoon objective. Enemy artillery was pinpointed to be eliminated by the heavy Allied artillery bombardment in the days preceding the attack. This time the Allied artillery would use high-explosive shells to destroy the big belts of German barb wire.

Most of the force of 100,000 men and 50,000 pack animals was hidden underground out of sight of the enemy's view from Vimy Ridge. The men and animals lived in huge tunnels to protect them and to deceive the enemy. There were so many that they were supplied by moving their provisions along 25 miles of underground tramways, and water for them was brought in by pipeline. Outside and above ground, the trenches themselves were knee deep in cold wet muck.

All was carefully timed beforehand for every participant. Every watch of every Canadian soldier had been synchronized before the attack. Before dawn many infantrymen stood in the cold, up to their waists in the mud, as they awaited the short furious three-minute artillery bombardment that would precede the signal to advance across No Man's Land to their designated objectives.

Precise artillery fire before the battle destroyed pre-plotted enemy artillery locations. During the attack the artillery would provide a creeping barrage that moved along in 100-yard steps. The infantrymen paced behind it, slogging through the mud and dodging the deadly craters, which were often as big as a house.

The advancing infantry had to be careful to remain behind their own creeping barrage or risk destruction from friendly fire as they avoided the craters in the cold slippery mud. They had practiced the "Vimy glide," the exact walking pace they needed to maintain so as to avoid fatally catching up to their own falling artillery barrage. Shells that fell short would be one more deadly hazard on this battlefield, but the steady pace forward had to be maintained by the infantry regardless of the casualties. They had exactly 35 minutes to reach their first objective.

Thain MacDowell believed in very careful study and preparation and would be spearheading the 38th Battalion's attack. He delighted in battle detail and is described as bringing to soldiering "a dedication of purpose and an implacable determination to master the crafts of battle." He studied this warfare methodically, and he went over the attack plans for Vimy Ridge over and over again. He knew his objectives so well that he had even picked out the enemy dugout where he would establish his company's new headquarters in the enemy trenches; but he could not know how many defenders were in it.

After being delayed by a day because of the wet weather, the attack began on Easter Monday, April 9, 1917. The infantry surfaced from underground and massed in the trenches for the coming attack across No Man's Land. A total of 983 heavy guns, howitzers, and mortars launched a barrage that lasted three minutes. At 5:30 a.m. they advanced in driving wind, snow, and sleet on a 7,000-yard frontage while the stormy northwest wind blew driving snow into the faces of the German sentries. The soldiers slogged up the ridge following closely behind the lethal creeping curtain of falling artillery shells which marched up the ridge 100 yards ahead of them. Sometimes they fell on their own advancing soldiers.

The infantrymen were upon the enemy trenches before the enemy soldiers could rise up from the bunkers in which they were sheltered from the artillery fire. By mid-afternoon the Canadian divisions were in command of the whole crest of the Ridge with the exception of two features known as Hill 145 and the Pimple. Within three days these were also captured, but the cost of victory among the four Canadian Divisions at Vimy was 10,602 casualties; other Allied forces there suffered further losses. The 4th Division had the most casualties, with one in three killed or wounded.

Victoria Cross

Four of the Canadians at Vimy Ridge, including Thain MacDowell, won the Victoria Cross medal, the highest award for gallantry in the face of the enemy that can be awarded to Canadian, British, and Commonwealth forces. Cast in bronze from cannons captured in the Crimean War at Sevastopol, Russia, the Victoria Cross bears a mystique that few other military decorations have ever attained. This most prestigious medal is awarded only to a select few. It is inscribed with just two telling words: "For Valour." Colonel MacDowell's is now displayed in the Soldiers Tower at the University of Toronto. The citation reads:

> For most conspicuous bravery and indomitable resolution in
> the face of heavy machine gun and shell fire. By his initiative
> and courage this officer, with the assistance of two runners,
> was enabled, in the face of great difficulties, to capture two
> machine guns, besides two officers and seventy five men.
> Although wounded in the hand, he continued for five days to
> hold the position gained, in spite of heavy shell fire, until
> eventually relieved by his battalion. By his bravery and
> prompt action he undoubtedly succeeded in rounding up a
> very strong enemy machine gun post.

Thain's battalion had been part of the force responsible to capture Hill 145, the highest part of the ridge, 475 feet above the surrounding plains. The advance to the enemy trenches was hard. In the confusion they had to bypass three large craters swarming with enemy soldiers, but in so doing their forces drifted to the right. When he reached the first enemy trench just before dawn, Thain was left with only two runners. Both would receive the Distinguished Combat Medal for their role in what occurred next.

Thain was about 50 yards to the right of the area he had aimed for, but most of his men had gone even farther to the right. He could see the dugout that he wanted for his company's headquarters, but he was under machine gun fire and could not take the time to collect his men. First he had to silence two German machine guns. He attacked one and overcame it with hand grenades but was wounded in the hand while doing this. Then he saw a defender retreating from the other machine gun and racing down into a dugout. He chased after him. Reaching the dugout, he found the steps stretched a long way down, underground.

He shouted for any Germans to come up and surrender but heard no response, so he climbed down 50 steps on a narrow stairway into the large underground dugout. As he rounded a comer, he came face to face with 77 Prussian Guards. Two were officers and 75 were soldiers who had been sent up as reinforcements to the front line the previous evening. He was alone. He looked back up the steps and shouted orders to an imaginary force in order to make them think that he was only the vanguard of a much larger force. The Prussian Guards raised their hands in surrender, but now he had to get his prisoners to the top of the dugout without them knowing he had only a force of three soldiers. His decision was to send the German soldiers up the steps in groups of 12. The first ones to reach the top realized they had been tricked. A German prisoner grabbed a discarded rifle and tried to shoot one of the two runners but missed and in return fire was then shot and killed, thus ending any further attempts at escape.

When Thain explored the captured dugout he found wires leading to five tons of high explosives planted in a tunnel and ready to be set off as a mine to kill the Allied attackers. All he could do was cut any visible wires and hang on to the position until sappers could come to his aid to defuse the five-ton mine beneath him. The dugout also contained good food, some very fine cigars, and Perrier water, which he said he enjoyed.

Soon the German machine guns and heavy artillery began pounding his location, but he was determined to hold such a fine military position, despite having no other officers or NCOs, with only a few men—some of whom were wounded, and low on guns and ammunition. Eventually that day he got help from 15 men, but their rifles were clogged with mud and they were of little help. His first dispatch at 10:30 a.m. reported his precarious situation.

> There are only 15 men with me of whom two are stretcher bearers. The rifles are one mass of mud, I have two Lewis Guns and only four pans. Both guns are out of action on account of the mud. We have a very few bombs as we had to bomb several dug outs.
>
> The 78th I have no trace of but there are two German Machine Guns just in front of us. They are firing constantly. Snipers are also busy. We cannot locate them as yet. The 72nd are on the left and seem to be spread out fairly well. The ground is practically impassible. His aeroplanes came over and saw a few of my men at dugout entrance and now we are getting his heavies from our right and his left. I have no N.C.O.'s whatever and unless I get a few more men with serviceable rifles, I hate to admit it, but we may be driven out. Three of the men are wounded as it is so I might as well tell you the facts of the case.

His third dispatch at 4:45 p.m. ended with this description of the heavy enemy artillery bombardment they were suffering in the captured dugout.

> His heavies are still pounding us but as yet have not hit any of
> the three entrances, but shakes the place.

He used his runners to carry dispatches and intelligence reports, to request reinforcements, and to request sappers to defuse the five-ton high-explosive mine in the underground tunnel below, as enemy artillery rained down shells upon them. He led his men to hold the dugout for five days until relieved by his battalion. His brave acts at Vimy Ridge had saved many lives.

He was invalided back to England where he received his Victoria Cross from King George V at Buckingham Palace. Then he was sent home on sick leave to Canada where he was hospitalized in Brockville for trench fever and shell-shock. His sister Eula, a nurse, at one point had to hold him down as he relived the terror of his experiences at Vimy Ridge. After sick leave he returned to England on March 1, 1918, where he served at the headquarters of the Overseas Military Force Canada and at the Canadian Training School.

After the War

On Armistice Day, November 11, 1918, the University of Toronto conferred an honorary Master of Arts degree upon Thain. On May 1, 1920, he was appointed brevet major of the Ottawa Regiment, the successor of his old regiment. He served as private secretary to the minister of National Defence from 1922 to 1928. In 1927 he was transferred to the reserve and appointed lieutenant colonel of the Frontenac Regiment in 1933.

Afterwards he made a career in engineering and became director of several mining companies as well as president of the Chemical Research Foundation.

In July, 1929, he married Norah Jean Hodgson of Montreal. They first lived in Toronto, but moved to Montreal in 1931. His wife died on November 1, 1983. They had two sons, Thain H. and Angus J. of Montreal.

In 1960, while alone in the Bahamas, he ignored pains that he thought were an upset stomach. Later his Nassau physician wrote to his sister about what had occurred, saying: "he was an active man and wanted to do important business" and so denied his "upset stomach." It was really a coronary heart attack and he died on March 27, 1960, in Nassau, the Bahamas.

Thain MacDowell was buried in Oakland Cemetery, Brockville, Ontario.

On Sept. 26, 1970, a memorial plaque in his honour was unveiled at the intersection of Highway 2 and Church Street in Maitland, just east of Brockville, Ontario:

Photo used with permission from the website www.ontarioplaques.com

He was a hero, and the Vimy Ridge battlefield is now the home of his nation's finest War Memorial to the soldiers of World War I.

MacDowell Descendants in Russia

Vitaliy Negoda (with Scott MacDougald)

I am Vitaliy Negoda and I live with my father Valeriy, my mother Maria, and my sister Anna in the city of Krasnodar near the northeast corner of the Black Sea in southern Russia. I was born in 1982. After I graduated from the law faculty of Kuban State University, I began work as a legal advocate in criminal cases, but my mother Maria dreams that someday I will become an international lawyer. She is a teacher in primary school with a degree from the Mathematics Faculty of Kuban State University.

My sister Anna was married in August 2005, and in February 2006 I became uncle to her little son, Alexander. Anna plans to graduate from the Kuban State Medical Academy next year. My father, Valeriy, graduated from two faculties of the Kuban State University—Mathematics and, later, Law. He works as a lawyer in Sberbank, in a private law practice.

Vitaliy Negoda

Sister Anna, nephew Alexander, Vitaliy, and mother Maria.

The life in Russia was not and is not very easy, but our family tried, and still tries, to preserve our pride and dignity. Part of our pride comes from my mother's MacDowell ancestors, who came from Ireland to Russia in the beginning of the 18th century. Since that time our family has lost much of what we knew about our MacDowell past, but I feel a strong kinship to them and a strong attraction to their traditions.

One thing our mother's family has passed down to us through the generations is a potted plant 30–35 centimeters (about a foot) in height. The shamrock-shaped leaves close up at night and open again in the morning. These leaves are green on one side but are as purple as ling heather on the other side. The flower blooms are purple, too. We believe that our mother's ancestors grew these plants to remind them of Ireland. Her family have always called it the "Good Morning" plant, but while writing this chapter I have finally discovered that this family heirloom has the scientific name of *Oxalis purpurea*, commonly named Purple Shamrock.

I first heard about the race of Celts when I was eight years old when we celebrated Halloween at school. Even in the Soviet period school holidays such as Halloween and St. Valentine's Day were celebrated. When my teacher told me about the Celtic origin of Halloween, something familiar about it touched my heart. From that time I began my research.

I had always noticed that my mother, her father Nickolay, and other kinsmen from my mother's side were different from the Slavonic Russians in their views and appearance. To me they seemed more noble, more honest, and more religious. They were ready to help not only their own children and parents, but were also ready to help other common people too. These are traits that you do not find every day in life here in Russia.

My mother Maria was born in 1960 and lived in the village of Belaya Glina before she moved 230 kilometers (144 miles) to Krasnodar to enter the University here. The village name "Belaya Glina" can be translated into English as "White Clay," because near the village there were large deposits of white clay. The village is situated in the north-eastern part of the Krasnodar Region. Our ancestors, the Laktionovs and the Mezentsevs, who intermarried with the MacDowells, have lived there since the foundation of the village in the mid-19th century. According to family tradition, before the mid-19th century the Laktionovs came from the Ukraine and the Mezentsevs came from the Ural Mountains to the village of Belaya Glina.

Cossacks lived in the Krasnodar Region, but in Belaya Glina lived other people from different parts of Russia and the Ukraine who were not the Cossacks. There was an area at the village, called Vorstadt by the Russian people, where there lived some men from far abroad. They were Germans, Dutch, and probably Irish. Vorstadt is a German word which was historically applied to settlements outside city walls.

In Czarist times before the Communist Revolution in Russia in 1917, my Laktionov family ancestors were rich farmers in Belaya Glina. They possessed lands near the village, had dozens of laborers and many cattle.

Also they had their family business in trading things made from the local white clay, which is good for making building materials and pottery.

My great-great grandfather was Mikhail Laktionov (or Michael in English). He had a brother Stefan, who was a well-educated man and a true gentleman. He knew some European languages and even Latin. Whenever Stefan went out of the house and walked down the streets of the village he wore his top hat, a jacket, and carried his walking stick. Our Russian peasantry had other traditions, and a lot of ordinary men were jealous of the wealth and manners of my ancestors. After the Communist Revolution in Russia in 1917, my ancestors' lands, cash, and money held in the banks were all confiscated by the Soviet authorities.

My ancestors, the Laktionovs and the Mezentsevs, were ardent Orthodox Christians and they were against the atheistic Soviet authorities during the Russian Civil War of 1918–1922. Stefan took part in the local riot against the Communists, but was unlucky. Firstly, the Communists wanted to hang him at the village square, but then Stefan was taken to prison, and since that time, nobody from our family has ever heard about him and his fate. My great-great-great grand-aunts from the Mezentsevs were forced to exile to Turkmenia in Asia for their religious views. One of these grand-aunts was named Hanna. After the end of the Civil War my ancestors were quiet citizens, but they preserved their Christian faith and their dignity.

My grandfather Nickolay was a bus driver and mechanic. He was the most noble and kind-hearted person whom I have ever met. He was always willing to help any relative. He had a custom of driving old people free of charge if they had no money. After the Second World War it was a very difficult time in the Russian countryside. Nickolay worked hard to earn money to pay for the higher education of his younger sisters, Zina and Svetlana, but he never took any higher education for himself. He died in 1997.

My sister Anna shared my connection for Celtic things. We were members of the Royal Scottish Country Dance Society for four years, where we danced as a demo-team. You can see two of our photos at http://puffball.demon.co.uk/krasnodar/. We danced together, but after her marriage and the birth of her son Alexander she has stopped Scottish dancing. When Fiona Grant, a well-known Scottish dance teacher from Bristol, England, was in our city of Krasnodar in September 2003, she told me that she strongly assumed that I was of Scottish origin. I had never told her about my MacDowell ancestors.

I feel a mystical connection with my MacDowell ancestors and the Ireland and Scotland in which they lived. My dream is to speak Gaelic well and to write poetry in the language of my ancestors. This connection has also taken me to studying and learning about the Gaelic language, the

MacDowell history, and the martial arts and warfare practiced in Ireland and in Scotland too.

In Ireland from about the year 1300 until about 1600 there was a famous and formidable class of mercenary warriors who came from the Hebrides islands and from the adjacent mainland territories of Scotland to fight in Ireland. They were called Gallowglasses. Of the six major family names of Gallowglasses, one was MacDowall and another was MacDougall (in Gaelic *MacDhughaill* or *O'Dubhghaill*) and they fought in the cause of the O'Connors against Anglo-Normans in Connacht.

Each Gallowglass had two servants to help carry his weapons and armor. The three of them were called a "sparth" after the five-foot-long Scottish sparth axe, which the Gallowglass used in battle to knock down charging enemy horses and their armored riders.

The Irish did not have experience fighting against the English armored forces, which had come to England with the Normans. The Irish usually fought with lightweight armor, which was no match for these armored cavalry brought against them by the English. The Scots had experience with this type of warfare and they had the weapons for it. The Gallowglass wore armor and his five-foot-long axe would bring down a horse and rider charging against him. Such formidable men were highly valued and highly paid. They earned three cows per quarter and lived on a diet of milk, meat, and cheese in a time when such a diet was out of reach of most people in Scotland and Ireland. They fought the English in Ireland for 300 years and were their most feared adversaries. Theirs was a long and famous martial tradition, but there are also old Celtic Martial Arts such as stick fighting, boxing, and various styles of wrestling.

I hope to open a school to teach these Celtic Martial Arts to others. That is a difficult challenge for me when I live so far away from other people who share a Celtic history and Celtic interests or have any Scottish or Irish heritage. I think that I can be helpful to my clan by opening my Clan MacDougall Gaelic Martial Arts School here in Russia. I have been practicing Celtic Martial Arts since December 2002 and since 2005 I have been a member of the Celtic Martial Arts Research Society and the Cateran Society. These organizations promote Scottish as well as Irish Martial Arts activities. You can read about them at www.geocities.com/cinaet/cumannbhata.html.

When I created the first Celtic wrestling event held here in April 2007—the Kuban Collar & Elbow Wrestling Tournament—Anna helped me to organize it. There is a funny story about that. Before the tournament Anna's husband Alexander had no Scottish-Irish connection and he was not a wrestler. He plays only soccer. At first he was not eager to take part in the event. But I told him that if you have a wife from such an honorable and warrior family as the MacDowalls, it is a shame not to take part. After the discussion he agreed to take part in the Wrestling Competition and he won the Silver Medal!

According to ancient Irish custom, the winner of the event has a right to choose the most beautiful girl to become May Queen of Beltane. The May Queen gives out the prizes and kisses to the winners. I feel that the saints—St. Andrew, St. Patrick, and St. Michael—all helped me to win that Wrestling Tournament. Because I had no true-love yet, I chose my sister Anna to be the May Queen.

In May and in June of 2007 two of the biggest local newspapers— the weekly "Krasnodar Evening," circulation 20,000, and the daily "Krasnodar News," circulation 33,000—published articles about my martial arts school. I am going to open my school in the summer of 2008 after finishing all training courses and preparing my instructors. In my school I want to teach students:

❖ Scottish and Irish stick fighting (*Bataireacht*)

❖ Gaelic swordsmanship

❖ various styles of Celtic wrestling (*Gleachd*, Collar & Elbow wrestling)

❖ Boxing and Highland athletics

Also in the school I am going to inform my students about our family history and the brave deeds of the MacDowall, MacDougall, and Doyle warriors.

I will name my school the "Clann Mhic Dhughaill Sgoil Iomairt Airm Gáidhlig Krasnodar," in honor of the noble kinsmen of MacDowall, MacDougall, and Doyle who bore the Gaelic name MacDhughaill or O'Dubhghaill in Ireland and Scotland.

Best wishes to all our kinsmen.

Vitaliy Negoda
Krasnodar, Russia

William L. MacDougall
Vitaliy at the Highland Games in Ligonier, Pennsylvania, in 2008.

Journeying in MacDowall Country

Walter M. Macdougall

A shower clears the afternoon of July 1, 1981. As the song goes, you can all but hear the angels sing in the sparkling waters of Larne on this glorious afternoon of warmish sunshine. The ferry is tethered to Ireland, but it points to Scotland, and we shall soon be on our way. The lines are cast off and with an escort of white gulls that sweep along the vessel's sides and swirl above our wake, we head eastward across the North Channel.

The Mull of Kintyre—you know the song, I'm sure—lies far to the north and is barely visible, and the mountains of Arran are half hidden in long, draping showers. The great cone of Ailsa Craig rises from the sea off the port bow, soon to be lost in a wall of rain. And now the high, bold hills of Galloway's shore grow taller in sun and shadow. High rock walls thread over these great hillsides, demarking pasturage dotted with sheep and cows. It looks as if we are running straight for this abrupt coast until the ferry swings right, and there is the long inlet of Loch Ryan leading to the port of Stranraer. The hillsides to the left are particularly grand, and one wonders if it was on such a dramatic day of weather that the MacDowells thwarted the invasion of Alexander and Thomas Bruce. Another quick shower as we land.

My first steps on British land and, in my naiveté, I walk past the telephone booth, unprepared for its bright red paint. My mistake corrected, a call brings the accommodating garage owner, himself, and the car which I am to rent. "It's simple enough," he told me in the midst of a brief driving lesson. "Remember, keep the passenger to the hedge." I soon found that this was an extremely helpful rule and easy to remember under stress even if one has no passenger.

Rhinns of Galloway

I head south down the Rhinns of Galloway. Roads are narrow and winding but well paved—like a driveway to an estate. There seems no place to park beside the pavement and take pictures, and when the road is not arched with trees, what panoramas open at each sharp turn and hilltop! The view of pasture tops and of the sea beyond cry out to be photographed on this, my first, evening in Scotland. Here I am in the *caput baroniae* of the Macdowalls of Garthland, and somewhere close by is Garthland Mains, where Garthland Castle stood from 1211 until 1848.

Walter M. Macdougall

The Rhinns of Galloway.

At Sandhead on the upper shore of Luce Bay, a village that marks the south bounds of the old barony of the McDowalls of Freugh, the long shadows remind me that I need to find a B&B for the night. The man I ask responds with a ready friendliness. He calls in to council a neighbor, and between the two there are many directions which would have been most helpful had I known as they did the names of the occupants of every chimney-potted cottage. Good fortune comes to my rescue and leads me to an inn on the shore of Port Logan. It is a small square building surrounded with what appeared to be a dry moat flanked by half-roofed remains of outbuildings. Its wider situation is grand—the ocean, evening-colored, rolling in on the sands of an arching bay. Having secured a room, I drive forth again as it is still light and the excitement seems electric.

The inner Rhinns is a country of immense, sweeping hillsides bright green with the July rows, gold and buff where the fields are newly mown with the hay bailed and piled. The long evening light of this land is flowing over a hundred shades of green and the crossings of the hedgerows. The undulating road is flanked with the campion and fox glove. The sounds are those of the sheep and the occasional voice of a cow or crow. Otherwise there is silence under the arching sky.

I stop on impulse at Kirkmaiden Church, which sits on a high hill surrounded by its cemetery stones. Here in the lingering, long light that is setting the world in amber, I find a tomb which keeps the dead of the MacDoualls of Logan who, as the inscription over the crypt door tells the passer-by, "for centuries held this land." They now rest in a beautiful spot of wide views—Luce Bay, the marches of Wigtownshire Peninsula, and far off, half hidden in the clouds which rise over Bruce's Carrick, the mountains of the Rhinn of Kells.

The road to the Mull of Galloway at the southern tip of the Rhinns becomes still narrower; it is a paved, twisting track, climbing and falling. With a surprising rumble, the car passes over a cattle grid and then the roadway is blocked by cows that, after an unhurried stare, get half a cow-length off the pavement. Two jack rabbits, seemingly all hind legs, are off in long bounds. Sheep are camera shy. There is a rainbow over the distant mountains of the Isle of Man which shares so much early history with the Macdowalls and the MacDougalls. Across the ocean to the south, the Cumberland hills of the English coast are clearly visible. To the east and north is Luce Bay, and beyond the bay 38 miles and amidst the highlands of Galloway, the Merrick rises blue, 2764 feet into bluer shower clouds.

I have reached the end of the land—the Mull of Galloway. Leaving the car, I walk to the edge of the great cliffs—or as near as I dare. I stand amidst the sheep; ahead there is only chasm and the sea, which beats in upon the rock many feet below. The cry of thousands of nesting sea birds is half human and half pre-human. To the left and at the very end of the hook of cliffs rises a tall lighthouse, its white tower gleaming in the last light against a background of lavender cloud.

As I return to the car, I meet a couple strolling in the cool of the evening. They hail from the old city of York and have parked their caravan on the crescent sands of East Tarbet, below the rocky bluffs where the Mull begins its final hook to the east. They have been trying without success to locate the site of the seaside chapel-cave of Saint Medan. In the storied days of the early saints, Medan arrived at the Mull of Galloway floating on a rock, and this gave rise to many miracles. Near the chapel she established were potholes worn in the rock by the sea. Sick children washed in the receptacles were made well.

Back at the inn, it seems that all the men and half the women in the neighborhood of Port Logan have come in for an evening drink—a tall glass of black beer for him and a shorter glass of yellow for her. Waiting for supper, I meet Willis Cameron. Willis is over from Canada and nostalgically reliving the days he spent at Port Logan as a boy. The War was raging then, and the bombing. He was sent with other children out of harm's way from Glasgow down to Galloway. It was all horses on the farms then and no running water. With the help of whiskey the memories are chasing each other. "Oh, it was hard discipline in those days. One was taught with a stick not to steal."

There was a ship of tea sunk off Port Logan. Bodies and cases washed in on the sands. The boys, hidden in an old, open-ended shed, tried to smoke the dried tea. Their teacher, a 70-year-old duffer pressed back into service for the duration of the war, was passing by and thought the shed was afire. He used his walking stick on them with good results.

My first night in Scotland! I open the window of my small upstairs room to the evening's half light. A breeze blows the curtains inward. Beyond the ruins of outbuildings, a hill rises abruptly to the fading sky. I lie embedded softly in a feather-filled mattress and pull up a layer of ample bedcovers. The sounds from the bar room below are muffled and pleasant. The green hills of Galloway stretch before the mind's eye—the rolling hills, the far-stretching sea, and the arch of cloud-filled sky. And this is only an appetizer, I am sure. I am in Scotland. Sleep comes easily on the wings of the evening wind.

Port Logan

MacDouall of Logan must have spent a fortune in his attempt to make Port Logan a principal shipping center and resort, with an eye on Irish traffic. Before breakfast and before the village is stirring, I go walking along the fine sand beach. The sea is washing in—one wavelet after the other darkening the sand—and the rising sun lights the green slopes of the Mull of Logan. My objective is to visit the tumble of quarried rock once intended for an extensive quay. It was Andrew MacDouall who started the construction in 1820; the same laird who was lampooned by Burns in *Ye Banks and Braes o' Bonnie Doon.* (If memory serves, jealousy over a woman was involved.)

The termination of the quay is still intact despite the seas that must beat upon it when the storms sweep in. The quay ends in a small stone lighthouse-like tower. There are no doors or windows. The small room within has a fireplace, a cupboard with a stone slab shelf, and in a cubicle the necessary facilities for a "two-holer." I wonder if this tower and the broken quay is all that is left of MacDouall's port of entry and make note that I must ask the innkeeper.

I have an opportunity to do so at breakfast, which includes a soup plate of oatmeal made at my request and brimming with cream. The landlord is very proud of his knowledge of American Indians and seems a bit disappointed that I am interested in local history; however, he promises to tell me about Port Logan before I depart. As he leaves me to eat my porridge, he turns and asks if I have signed the guest book. There is something about the police checking now and then on aliens from Ireland, only 18 miles away.

I have about finished breakfast when I hear my landlord speaking in the hallway to a new arrival. The voices are low, but at the end of the conversation, I distinctly hear the new arrival say, "Let me know if he stays about." I had felt eyes watching me when I was on my morning exploration and as I jotted in my little notebook and took photos. Evidently that impression was correct.

The bill for my stay is presented on a silver tray, and then the innkeeper kindly sits down at the table to tell me the story of the inn and of Port Logan, all of which has much to do with local MacDouall history. I could not have been more fortunate in my search for information. The inn was built by Macdouall of Logan as the harbormaster's house. Had I noticed the projecting stones at each gable? It was intended that the house would be connected to a range of buildings including stables and a hotel, all of which would face the beach in a crescent. What I had taken for ruins were, in fact, the foundations for these additional structures. The grand scheme had scarcely begun when the troubles started.

"Have you noticed," the innkeeper asks, "that the line of cottages beyond the inn are fronted with a raised road around the harbor so that their view of the shore and bay is obstructed?" It seems that MacDouall tried to get the fishermen who owned the cottages to sell and make room for the expanding resort. He built several model homes behind the line of cottages and higher up the hill, offering these as inducements, but the fishermen would not budge. He then built a new road before their front yards, elevated to cut off their access to the beach, but they still would not give in. The descendants of those fishermen probably still live in the cottages walled off from the bay.

Logan House

I do not visit another of MacDouall's contrivances in the form of a fish pool where wild codfish wait to be stroked. Instead I set off to find Logan House. In a short time it is obvious that better directions are needed. These are provided by a friendly sheep farmer with whom I exchange climatic data. It seems that the Rhinns of Galloway seldom have snow and that palm trees can be grown. I am soon to see proof of this. Arriving by roads not on my map, as nearly as I can tell, I come to a stop beside the once ornate, red sandstone gables of the Logan estate. Across the roadway, tall palm trees rise above a high stone wall.

My good fortune continues. As I step out of the car, there is a regal pheasant feather lying at my feet, and I soon meet a retired gardener with clear blue eyes under shaggy brows and equally prominent pride in the extensive and exotic botanic garden of the Logan estate, which I learn is managed by the Royal Botanic Garden in Edinburgh.

The Laird is away from the big house, I am told, but "disregard the 'strictly private sign' at the entrance to the drive and you will find Willy McKinley, the gardener at the mansion. He'll surely give you permission to take photographs."

Fergus D. H. Macdowall

Logan House without its original wings.

The present Logan House was built in 1702, after a fire in 1500 burned "Balzieland" Castle, held so long and in trying times by the MacDoualls. A fragment of wall from this castle has survived, surrounded now by the garden. The new house, like the stables I had seen earlier, is made of red sandstone. Stone stairs rise from a raised lawn to the front door, and the house itself presents a solidarity topped with large chimneys. Willy was on his "holiday," but I found a John McHerrie, a gentleman carpenter with frock and tie along with his helper. Mr. McHerrie lives in Ardwell nearby and is, as I soon learn, a local historian and very proud of the countryside. He was most willing to tell me about the MacDoualls of Logan.

According to McHerrie, one MacDouall laird was in competition for a fair lass with the owner of a neighboring estate. He was winning the contest and returning from a courting visit when his adversary loosed his hounds upon his competition. A stone engraved with the word *Murder* marks the spot where MacDouall was overtaken. Fergus D. H. Macdowall of Garthland assures the writer that this is a tale born of wild imagination,* but it does prove that this countryside is rich with folklore. I wonder as McHerrie tells this tale if Arthur Conan Doyle had heard this story or one much like it and from it spun *The Hound of the Baskervilles.*

McHerrie's stories continue. Smuggling salt appears to have been a major occupation in Galloway. On one occasion when the officers entered a cottage, they found a woman upon her childbed and in great agony. When they left, the woman was delivered of the salt bags upon which she had been lying.

---

* Fergus D. H. Macdowall of Garthland gives an account that may have been twisted into this tale, in the Fall 1989 edition of *The Tartan.*

Glenluce Abbey and Beyond

I am told that *Glenluce* means the "Glen of light" and that often when all around the countryside is gray, a shaft of light will illuminate this spot. Then McHerrie's wife will remark, "Ah, there is Glenluce living up to its name." This is a wonderful country full of history, says McHerrie. He sharpens his carpenter's pencil with a chisel and takes down my address in a notebook filled with jottings. He may be able to send more information, and he did.

Glenluce lies to the east of the Rhinns of Galloway, on the way to Newton Stewart. In 1190, Roland, the fourth Lord of Galloway and brother of Duegald from whom the Macdowalls and all the Galloway MacDowells take their name, founded Glenluce Abbey. The arms of this ancient line can still be seen in the ceiling of the Chapter House. It spattered rain as I left the Abbey, but this was only a clearing shower, and I drove eastward in a day of clouds piled on the horizon, of cirrus feathering the blue arch, and of views of shining sea and pleasant hills.

One needs to have made a serious study of the geography and history of a particular area in order to discover what it has to offer. I learned only later that Machrimore Castle, which was held by the Macdowalls until 1600, still stands at Newton Stewart. More than that, it is still occupied, which is amazing in this land where the iron rams of war and the relentless havoc of time have left so little standing.

As I travel, I realize how deeply the roots and associations of the Macdowalls (in all their spellings of that surname) are interlaced with this wide countryside of Galloway. Evidently one needs much more than several days to make a meaningful pilgrimage. At Newton Stewart, I have a conference with a lady in the information booth and decide I must forgo driving northward to Glen Trool. I will not see the wildest part of Galloway amidst the mountains of the Rhinn of Kells, where MacDougalls from Lorn and the Macdowalls hunted for Robert the Bruce. I still regret not exploring a place with place names such as The Murder Hole, Loch of Ambush, and *Pulmaddy* ("Wolf's Burn").

Instead I head south by west along the shore of Wigtown Bay to the Gate House of Fleet, where I stop to buy bread and fruit. Nearly 700 years ago, King Edward I of England also gathered supplies here and appointed Dougal Macdowall Sergeant of Galloway with the commission of apprehending all intruders. I hope that clan affiliation will offer me some security in this town of grim reminders. The town now surrounds the castle where Claverhouse, known in the Highlands as "Bonnie Dundee," stayed during the "killing times." It is a dark ruin of chimneys, ragged gables, and black window holes. Not far away, the old tollbooth where John Paul Jones was once a prisoner still has its chain and neck ring hanging on the outside wall near the door.

Not knowing what is around the next bend in the road produces exciting encounters, and the sudden appearance of Cardoness Castle rising from a ridge above the road is such an experience. Cardoness was the seat of the MacCullochs. As far as I know, the only connection with the Macdowalls is the marriage (1453) of Patrick Macdouall of Logan to a daughter of Sir Alexander MacCulloch, but it is Cardoness' state of preservation which is important to this journal. As has been suggested, it is rare to find an old stronghold still standing in the Macdowall country.

My immediate impulse is to scale the heights and reach the castle, but nettles and fence foil the attack, and when I follow the road to the other side of the old tower, there is a welcoming parking lot. Roses in profusion grow on the walls of the old kitchen, and there are tours and brochures. Cardoness, as it stands, is a great, square tower four stories high with the remains of the gables above that. It has all the important features including a murder hole over the doorway and a bottle prison entered from the top through a one and a half foot grate.* The hall is a rock-enclosed, empty space of echoes, but there are remnants of red sandstone fireplace surrounds, with gothic pillars and decorated moldings for cupboards.

Kirkcudbright and its surrounding countryside is my next destination. It plays an important part in Macdowall history. Bombie, Twynholm, and Borgue were all once lands belonging to the name, and above the town was located Fergus of Galloway's Palace Isle. Stone taken from that center of lordly power was used to build Kirkudbright Castle, which was constructed by Macdowall allies, the Maclellans. Kirkudbright is associated with Cuthbert, the shepherd boy who became a saint. His followers stayed here when, with the Saint's sacred bones, they rested during their flight from the marauding Danes. A few miles to the east lies the Abbey of Dundrennan, that sacred place long noted for its sense of peace.

Dundrennan

The finest medieval ruins of Galloway are its abbeys.† I round a bend in the bright sunshine and there, astonished, awe-filled in fact, look down upon Dundrennan framed by the roadside trees and sunning its ruddy stones on green lawns by the side of a stream.

---

* The guide thought that this feature may have served as a means of raising food from the outside kitchen to the hall.
† The abbey at Glenluce has been mentioned, but there is also Sweetheart Abbey where Devorgilla of Galloway lies buried along with her husband, John Baliol.

With the encouragement of King David I, Fergus, Lord of Galloway, built this Abbey in 1142, and here Alan, the last Lord of Galloway, lies buried. The abbey is, according to the books, New Gothic in style. It was constructed under the supervision of John Murdow, master mason, who also superintended the building of Saint Andrews, the High Kirk of Glasgow, as well as Melrose and Paisley Abbeys. The inscription to his memory ends with an introit to God, Mary, and "sweet Saint John." Saint John, the patron saint of masons, would be moved by Dundrennan, for there is beauty here even in its ruins—especially in the rhythm of its repeated pointed arches, the huge supporting columns carved to look like bundles of smaller shafts, and the high windows of the south transept illuminated with the clear depth of the blue sky. The vaulted cells which once housed Cistercian monks are now the repository for fragments of sculptured pieces: trefoils, shields and groin work all piled together. One old stone with artistic simplicity yet elegance shows a woman with a high Elizabethan collar. For a long moment I stand silent remembering that Mary Queen of Scots spent her last night in Scotland here at Dundrennan, but even this sad thought is melted away by resplendent afternoon. The sun-warm ruins are a fitting place for a festival with bright streamers and song.

I have one other encounter before leaving Dundrennan Abbey. I come upon him quite suddenly, the life-size effigy of an abbot. He stands in a narrow alcove, wrapped in a long many-pleated habit and peering with eyes intense yet without pupils. His right fist rests upon his chest while his left hand holds his long crosier diagonally across his body. His feet pins down a small male figure. Is this the devil, the abbot's lesser self, his faithful dog, or some worldly and bested enemy?

Buittle Castle

My next objective is Buittle Castle, the Scottish home of John Baliol; his wife Devorgilla, Lady of Galloway; and their son King John I of Scotland, who figured largely in the world of the MacDougalls and the Macdowalls. The location of this castle is in a valley and beside Urr Water, which on this day flows bluer than the sky above. As I ease the car down a precipitous road, there appears below an unusual site—not a castle but a lived-in tower house with tall gray walls and two small dormers in the steep slate roof. The daughter of this restored house was charmingly helpful. The tower house, like most of its type, dates from the 16th century. It originally had a turret on one of its upper corners where now there is a bit of corbel left. A print hanging in the hallway shows the tower before restoration. It is roofless, and the lass explains that as long as there was no roof owners avoided taxes—a common practice in Scotland. But now, once more, the tower house is very much a home, with smoke coming from its chimney, surrounded with cows, and a cow byre standing close by.

The remains of the Buittle Castle are owned by Oxford University, which was endowed by the Baliols. Its remains lie on a knoll to the east of the tower house. I make my way as directed, past the staring cows and over a small burn, which was once part of the castle's moat and now is hidden among waist-high nettles, a blue weed, and the purple spikes of foxglove. There is not much left of this proud old place, at least above ground. Its mound is overgrown with ivy-twined trees. Here and there I find what I take to be the remains of stone foundations. There is a poetic touch in the intermingling of foxglove and purple-flowered nightshade growing together in the dense vegetation where once the stronghold of so much ambition stood.

> Foxglove and nightshade side by side
> Emblems of punishment and pride.

> ~ Sir Walter Scott

The day had become more splendid as the hours passed. My memories include the impression of tree-arched roads, narrow between the hedges and turning in the sun and shade; and of hamlets with single lines of cottages, blue, white, and even pink, all with chimney pots and front doors close to the street. There are high-climbing and bald-topped hills and valleys with clear streams running below arched bridges. And so I drive back through the lovely country of Galloway to Stranraer.

❋ ❋ ❋

The lodging I find is a room under the eaves with a roof light for its window, which opens like a hatch so that I can see out across the rooftops and feel the cool evening breeze blowing from the harbor. Across the street another B&B is evidently filled with girls; their laughter and songs are delightful and add a youthful lilt to memories of beautiful, old Galloway.

MacDowalls of Note

William L. MacDougall

From warriors to ministers and actors to educators, the MacDowalls have produced many illustrious sons and daughters in addition to the ones mentioned earlier.

Sir Walter Scott, Author

Particularly in the field of arts and letters, the family has been especially gifted. One of the most famous of all MacDowell descendants was Sir Walter Scott, novelist and poet, whose works helped to establish the framework for fiction in the 19th and 20th centuries, and whose influence is still felt.

Born in Edinburgh in 1771, he was the great-great grandson of Anne Isobel MakDougall of Makerstoun and Walter Scott. The MacDougalls (also spelled MakDougall) of Makerstoun are the senior cadet—meaning branch—of the MacDowalls of Garthland. Sir Walter was made aware of that proud inheritance in childhood.[*]

Sir Henry Raeburn, 1822

Many of his novels, such as *Waverley* and *Redgauntlet*, reflect his intimate knowledge of the turbulent history of Scotland. He was influential in his later years in promoting Scottish culture, and helped to reverse the once-powerful tide of South British resentment against the Scots for wars with the English.

In 1818, Sir Walter was awarded a baronetcy by the Prince Regent. He built an estate at Abbotsford, near Melrose (close to Makerstoun), where he died in 1832. His novels are still widely read, and continue to influence fiction into the 21st century.

---

[*] Scott's achievements are also noted in the Makdougals of Makerstoun chapter.

Edward MacDowell, Musician

Another descendant who made his mark on the arts was Edward MacDowell, the composer. He was born in New York in 1861, and was recognized early for his musical gifts. The United States in the 19th century offered little in the way of musical education, so he was sent to France at age 15 for studies at the Conservatoire of Paris. His classmates included such future luminaries as composer Claude Debussy. He later transferred to conservatories in Frankfurt and Stuttgart, where he was heavily influenced by the German school of music and such contemporaries as Johannes Brahms.

One of the musical superstars of the period, Franz Liszt, was greatly impressed by MacDowell's early works. Liszt introduced the American to other European artists and audiences.

When MacDowell returned to the United States in 1888, he announced that he wanted to help establish serious music throughout America. He wrote a number of major works, including two piano concertos, which are still performed, and a considerable number of songs such as "To a Wild Rose" and "To a Water Lily." He was the first head of the department of music at Columbia University.

Grove's Dictionary of Music and Musicians, 1907

Some critics complained that MacDowell was more Celtic than American, but he considered himself an advocate of New World music. "What we must arrive at," he said, "is the youthful optimistic vitality and the undaunted spirit that characterize the American man. That is what I hope to see achieved in American music."

He was widely heralded at the turn of the last century as the most distinguished American composer of serious music. Since then, his reputation has diminished, but he is still considered one of the most important of the nation's early composers.

Harold C. Schonberg, former senior music critic of the *New York Times*, wrote of MacDowell: "Through his activities as a composer of world-wide reputation, and as pianist and as teacher, he crystallized an emergent national pride." MacDowell died in 1908. His widow founded the MacDowell Colony, an artists' center, in Peterborough, New Hampshire.

Sir Arthur Conan Doyle, Author

Arthur Conan Doyle was born in Edinburgh in 1859, into the Irish-Scottish Doyle family, which is connected to the MacDowalls.

He at first became a physician, but was more interested in writing, and devoted himself full-time to that craft after the success of his first work about the fictional detective, Sherlock Holmes. He died in 1930. His novels remain among the best-read fiction in the world.

New York Times

MacDowall Actors

The family also has been blessed with a substantial number of distinguished actors. One such performer is **Malcolm McDowell**, who has appeared in dozens of movies, stage plays, and television dramas.

He was born in England in 1943. His name at birth was Malcolm John Taylor, but in adulthood he discovered there was already an actor by that name in the Screen Actors Guild, which allows only one person per name. So Malcolm adopted his mother's maiden name, McDowell, by which he has achieved his fame.

He was an avid athlete, playing both rugby and cricket, and worked in jobs such as coffee salesman and waiter in his parents' pub before trying his hand at acting. He was encouraged by a teacher of elocution who heard him speaking and said he had a "marvelous voice."

McDowell played on stage in repertory companies in small cities in England before being accepted by the Royal Shakespeare Company in 1964. But he chafed under a routine that required younger actors to accept tiny parts and move scenery in support of older, more established players.

He appeared in television roles, and received a major break when he was hired in 1968 for a role in the movie, "If..." The film was widely acclaimed, although not a big box-office success, and he was then selected for a leading part in "A Clockwork Orange." That role firmly established him as a major international star.

Since then, he has performed in a wide variety of roles in films such as "Caligula," "Time After Time," and "My Life So Far." He is considered to be among the world's most talented and versatile actors even in his fifth decade in the business.

Another well-regarded performer is **Andie MacDowell**, actor and former fashion model, born in Gaffney, South Carolina, in 1958.

As a teenager, she worked at McDonald's and Pizza Hut stores. She dropped out of college when her good looks were spotted by a modeling agency, and she was placed in advertising for cosmetic and clothing manufacturers. She appeared in small parts in movies in the 1980s, and won an important role in "Sex, Lies, and Videotape."

Since then, she has appeared in leading roles in films such as "The Object of Beauty," "Groundhog Day," and "Four Weddings and a Funeral."

Roddy McDowall was another star with a long career in movies. Born in London in 1928, he was the son of a merchant mariner and a mother who wanted to be an actor.

His movie career started in 1938, with "Murder in the Family," and continued the rest of his life until his death in 1998. Near the start of World War II, his mother brought him to the United States, where he found prominent roles and childhood stardom.

He had starring parts in such famous movies as "My Friend Flicka," "Lassie Come Home," "Cleopatra," "Funny Lady," "Evil Under the Sun," and "How Green Was My Valley." He also appeared in plays and won a Tony award in 1960.

McDowall confessed he was not always comfortable with animals in movies. He said: "I really liked Lassie, but that horse, Flicka, was a nasty animal with a terrible disposition."

Sir Anthony Dowell, Dancer

In the field of ballet, a prominent figure is Sir Anthony Dowell, a premier dancer on the stage and a choreographer and director.

He was born in London in 1943, and studied at the Royal Ballet schools. He joined the Royal Ballet in 1961 and was chosen for his first starring role in "The Dream" only two years later. He rose quickly to become a principal dancer. He had major parts in such ballets as "A Month in the Country," "Enigma Variations," "Manon," "Cinderella," and "Romeo and Juliet." Many roles were created for him by choreographers including Frederick Ashton, Kenneth MacMillan, and Antony Tudor.

Dowell's fame spread quickly across the world, and he became a featured performer with the American Ballet Theatre in the United States. He also danced with the National Ballet of Canada and the Joffrey Ballet.

He was appointed director of the Royal Ballet in 1986. He was named Commander of the Order of the British Empire in 1972 and a Knight Bachelor in the Queen's birthday honors list. In 1994, Sir Anthony was honored with the Royal Academy of Dancing's Queen Elizabeth II Coronation Award.

Other MacDowall Professionals

Michael McDowell is a former Tanaiste (Deputy Prime Minister), Attorney General, and Minister for Justice, Equality and Law Reform of the Republic of Ireland. He was also the leader of the Progressive Democrat Party. He was born in Dublin in 1951.

W. Stuart McDowell is a producer, composer, playwright, and educator. Born in St. Louis in 1947, he is a founder of the Riverside Shakespeare Company in New York. He has directed many plays on a variety of stages, including "Romeo and Juliet," "Hamlet," "Show Boat," "Cyrano de Bergerac," and "The Crucible."

He is a former Fulbright Scholar and the winner of the Kennedy Center's American College Theater Festival Direction and Playwriting award. He has been chairman of the department of theater, dance, and motion pictures of Wright State University in Dayton, Ohio, since 1994.

Dr. John C. McDowell is the Meldrum lecturer in systematic theology at the School of Divinity of the University of Edinburgh. Born in Northern Ireland, he studied at the University of Aberdeen and is a member of the Church of Scotland's Panel of Doctrine.

He is author of *The Gospel According to Star Wars: Faith, Hope and the Force* and co-editor of *Conversing with Barth*.

Jennifer McDowell is a sociologist, composer, playwright, and publisher. She is editor and publisher of Merlin Papers in San Jose, California, and was a composer for Paramount Pictures, co-producer of a radio show, and a poet. She also is co-creator of the musical comedy, "Russia's Secret Plot to Take Back Alaska."

❋ ❋ ❋

In the first years of the second millennium, the MacDowalls have a proud history of achievement in many fields. And there is every reason to believe the seeds have been planted for many more contributions to advancement in the future.

The spirit, if not the letter, survives of those hardy MacDowall Scots who proudly proclaimed their motto in battle, "Victory or Death."

Castles, Towers, and Other Fortifications

Scott A. MacDougald, Walter M. Macdougall,
and Fergus D. H. Macdowall

In Galloway the Latin *castella* or Gaelic *caiseal* (pronounced "castle") were the words generally applied to any strong house of stone. While most of the medieval defensive domiciles in Galloway were called "castles," it is useful for descriptive purposes to categorize them as castles, keeps, tower houses, or peles.

Types of Structures

Castle—A rectangular enclosure of considerable size having halls, kitchens, and other accommodations built against the inside of the perimeter curtain walls. Advances in design over time led to rounded corner towers rather than the older Norman square towers of shallow projection. *Motte and bailey* castles were popular on the Borders in Norman times, but the *ring work* model was also common. These 11th and 12th century castles of earthwork and timber were relatively cheap and simple to build, although generally short-lived. However, some survived for centuries by being renewed with timber or stone materials. Fergus Lord of Galloway adopted yet another castle model for additional defensive protection, with his palace surrounded by the water of Lochfergus. His "Palace Isle" was built in the midst of a loch like the crannogs of ancient inhabitants of Galloway but his castle was made of stone, and it had a submerged secret causeway to the entrance.

Keep—A strong tower within the walls of a fortress. Another name for a keep is "donjon." Keeps feature a single tower with the kitchen, hall, and living quarters on successive vertical levels. Keeps usually had outworks, including a postern entrance and enclosed courtyard or bailey. Keeps were often built of stone and located on an eminence or motte, which was frequently artificially built up higher with excavated materials.

Palace—An old Scottish term for the two-story hall, block domestic building of a high-status person such as a bishop or royalty. Such high-status buildings had some defensive fortifications but they were not military forts.

Pele or **Peel**—A fortified house built with some defenses such as free-standing towers, or built with towers attached to other unfortified buildings. Peles with stockades were more common in Scotland. A pele on Heston Island was held by Duncan Macdowyll of Garthland during the Scottish Wars of Independence.

Tower House—A simpler form of keep, often built with a vaulted cellar at ground level and with the entrance on the second story. Later constructions were much more ornamented.

Glossary of Structural Elements

Abatis—A defensive perimeter formed by a mass of felled trees whose sharpened branches face the enemy to obstruct their ability to approach the outer walls.

Bailey—The space enclosed by the outer wall of a castle. It can be called a courtyard. In Scotland only the most important castles had a bailey.

Fosse—A ditch or moat that restricts the enemy's approach to the outer walls of a fortification. It may contain water.

Harled wall—An exterior wall covered by a surfacing technique used to weatherproof stone buildings such as Scottish castles. A slurry of small pebbles or fine chips of stone is thrown (hurled) onto a wet lime surface on the stone, then lightly pressed into it.

Interiors—While the first floor halls were usually paved with stone supported upon the vaults of the cellar, the upper floors were made of wood resting on joists running from stringers along the walls that, in turn, rested on projecting corbels. In some cases floor joists were mortised into the walls themselves.

Moat—A type of fosse. It is a deep wide trench dug around a fortification and usually filled with water.

Mote or **motte**—A hill, often man-made with materials excavated from the fosse around it, to give added height to the buildings being constructed upon it. On some motes, ring work fortifications were built. Their defensive structures were usually wooden until the advent of stone-built keeps.

Mote Hill or **Moot Hill**—A flat-top hill or an unfortified mound for courts of justice. There are several in Galloway. The word "mote" is believed to be from the Gaelic word *mod* meaning a council or court of justice.

Postern—A secondary door or gate at the back or side.

Roofs—The roofs were supported on timber bents, while the gables were of stone, often with the characteristic "crow step" construction, which results in a stair-like appearance. Early roofs were covered with turf or timber, and many later ones with lead or slates.

Walls—The thick walls of earlier castles and tower houses were built of roughly coursed and unsquared stones. Corners and openings were dressed with squared blocks of sandstone. Door and window facings were often carved and chamfered. Portals, windows, embrasures, and passageways were either capped with large stone mantels or arched.

Huge timber lintels were also employed, harking back to earlier building practices.

Macdowall Fortifications

Fortified dwellings were used by the Macdowalls for centuries after the time of Fergus of Galloway. This section describes the fortifications of the MacDowells of Galloway. Where possible, the stirp (branch) or cadet associated with each fortification is included in the description. The following list shows the three stirps of the MacDowalls with their cadets listed underneath their names. These are mostly names of farmlands and estates and are not feudal baronies or castles except for Macdowall of Machrimore, Makdougall of Makerstoun, Macdowall of Mindork, Macdowall of Castlesemple, and Macdowell of Stodrig.

Macdowall of Garthland
Macdowall of Castlesemple*
Macdowall of Corochtrie
Macdowall of Crookuncrush
Macdowall of Elrig (at times)
Macdowall of Knockglass
Macdowall of Lefnall
Macdowall of Machrimore
Makdougall of Makerstoun**
Macdowall of Mindork
Macdowall of Myroch
Macdowell of Stodrig**

McDouall of Logan
McDouall of Ardwell
McDouall of Crichton
McDouall of Culgroat
Macdowall of Dalreagle
McDouall of Elrig (at times)

McDouall of Freugh
McDouall of Hackburn
McDouall of Stratford Hall
McDouall of Killaster
McDouall of Longcaster

     * Located in Renfrewshire
     ** Located in Roxburghshire

**MacDowall Stirps and Cadets Occupying Castles
and Fortified Places of Galloway**

Auchness Castle

Origin—This is a tower house dating from around 1600. The name is said to derive from the Gaelic as a compound from the Gaelic *Achadh* and the Norse *nes* meaning "the field at the point." It was the property of the McDoualls of Logan. In 1621 Alexander M'Dowall, Laird of Logan, settled the lands of Auchness upon his bride, Jane Agnew, as part of her dower. It is said that the castle served as a jointure house for the widows of the adjoining lairdship of Logan. In the 17th century the McDoualls of Ardwell were on record as a cadet of the McDoualls of Logan.

Location—In the Parish of Kirkmaiden in Wigtownshire, about 9 miles south of Stranraer, on a minor road west of Route A716. It is ½ mile west of Luce Bay and 1 mile south of Ardwell, on the Rhinns of Galloway.

Description—The three stories and a garret of the old tower house were much altered and modernized into a farm house in the 19th century with additions to the north, south, and west sides. It measures about 20 feet square with walls 3 feet thick. Its walls have a harled exterior and most of the windows have been enlarged. It is oblong on plan, with a steep roof and with modern dummy turrets crowning three angles. The gables are crow-stepped.

Barr Castle

Origin—This was built by 1525 by the Glens of Barr. They were a family who had held the Lordship of Glen from the time of David I until it was given to the Abbey of Paisley in 1292. Afterwards they held the barony of Barr. "Barr" is from the Gaelic for "hilltop dweller." In 1509 the estate boundaries were disputed by the nearby Semples, who built a pele on an island in the loch. The Glens built Barr Castle as a defensive fortification and later added a courtyard with a gun slot aimed at the Semples. When the Glen line failed in the early 17th century, Barr Castle was acquired by John Wallace, a

Fergus D. H. Macdowall
Barr Castle in 1930

son of Wallace of Elderslie, forbearers of the famed William Wallace. John Wallace was descended from the Wallaces of Riccarton, as were the Macdowalls of Gairochloyne. He married Margaret Hamilton, and their son took the name Hamilton of Barr. From the late 16th to late 18th centuries Barr Castle was owned by the Hamiltons. After 1780, when the Macdowalls acquired the Barr and Garpel lands, the Hamiltons paid them feu duties until the Hamilton line ended without progeny in the 19th century. Professor Fergus Day Hort Macdowall has his "seat" at Barr Castle.

Location—The castle stands about 1 mile west of the village Lochwinnoch in the parish of Lochwinnoch in Renfrewshire and is visible from Route A760. The castle is situated in the policy park south of Barr Wood to the south of Barrbank on the Kilbirnie Road. It stands on the Garthland estate, formerly the Barr-Garpel estate, in parkland overlooking Barr meadow and Barr Loch.

Description—This ruined four-story tower measures 35 feet by 25 feet. It had a courtyard on the west and south sides, and a gunport on the north side. The parapet has fallen from the structure. There was once a two-story outbuilding on the south side. There is evidence of alterations made in 1680 and 1699 to the original construction. The new ground-floor entrance leads onto a passage connecting a vaulted cellar in the south end to the kitchen on the north side, but the original entrance was high in the west wall.

Fergus D. H. Macdowall

Barr Castle with Barr Loch in the background

Buittle Castle

Origin—The old spelling (and correct pronunciation) is "Botel," derived from the Anglo-Saxon word *botl*, a "dwelling" in the Norse and Saxon languages. Excavations have found building remains dating back to around 1150. These had been destroyed and built over more than once. Buittle or Botel Castle was probably the successor of a wooden tower surrounded by palisade fortifications that stood on the site now known as Motte of Urr, half a mile upstream.

Originally Botel was a stronghold and a favorite residence of the Lords of Galloway. About 1230 Alan of Galloway built a courtyard castle here on a large 12th century motte. After Dervorgilla's marriage to John Baliol it passed to the Baliols. John Baliol's favorite Scottish residence is said to have been Botel, upon which he liberally expended the ample revenues from his English estates. It became the chief seat of the Baliol family in Scotland. Dervorgilla is credited with doing much construction at Botel. She occupied it until her death in 1290. In September 1296, after the abdication of King John Baliol, Botel Castle was committed by King Edward I to the keeping of Henry de Percy. Botel now became an English royal fortress. After Bruce invaded Galloway, Botel was the only garrison that held out against him until he captured it on March 31, 1313; Bruce ruined it after its surrender to him. He presented the castle to the Good Sir James Douglas in 1324, subject to the yearly tribute of one pair of spurs.

After victory at the battle of Halidon Hill in July 1333, the claimant King Edward Baliol resumed residence at Buittle. Supported by MacDoualls and MacCullochs after the English victory at Durham in 1347, Baliol maintained a residence here and did reconstruction work on the castle. In 1353 he was forced out by a strong force under Sir William Douglas (Lord) of Douglas. Buittle Castle was left a ruin under the care of Oxford University. It is not to be confused with Buittle Place, an L-plan tower built nearby, now restored as a farmhouse.

Location—In the parish of Buittle in Wigtownshire, one mile west of Dalbeattie, on a small mount in the valley of the Urr Water on the western bank of the river. Buittle Castle is situated off Route A745, 13 miles northeast of Alston, on Route A686, in a very pleasant spot in the valley of the Urr Water. The site is owned by the National Trust.

Description—Buittle Castle is one of four Norman castles in Galloway. Nowadays Old Buittle Farmhouse is built near the site of Buittle Castle. The castle's vaults and traces of fortification are all that remain of the original large and impressive structure. The present site shows visible earthworks and ruins.

It was an Edwardian-type castle, with curtain walls enclosing a space of about 150 by 100 feet. Massive round towers projected at the wall angles. The main entrance was in the northwest, likely at a drawbridge. A deep ditch or moat around the castle has since been converted to a roadway on the north and west outer slopes. A plateau to the northwest forms a bailey of 500 by 300 feet. Excavations of the fosse north of the bailey found two stone walls and a massive buttress that could have formed the base for a drawbridge or gateway leading from the south bailey to a smaller north bailey, which could have been an animal pen. The defensive perimeter of the south bailey has evidence of long dismantled defenses, including a massive timber palisade on the south and east sides. On the north side, a deep fosse had been dug through the bedrock to form a U-shaped ditch with a stone wall to the south and an abatis to the north.

In the south bailey was a two-story L-shaped Mansion House constructed by Edward Baliol in 1347, with stone walls up to 4 feet thick. It may have been constructed with its stone walls up to 6 feet high supporting timber paneling that rose up to roof level. The roof was made of timber or turf. There is evidence of ruins of earlier buildings beneath it that date to about 1150.

On the north side of the site are the remains of an artificial mound, along the edge of the ravine. North of the moat and west of the river bank, excavations found evidence of massive military fortifications that had been burned down. These had consisted of two square timber towers two stories high and a timber palisade. There were stables set in behind the timber-palisaded perimeter defenses on the south and east sides. On the riverbank there are still traces of a harbor or landing place with the capacity to hold several small craft. Artifacts found at the site during archaeological digs are in the Stewartry Museum in Kirkcudbright.

Castle Balzieland (Balzieland Tower, Logan Tower)

Origin—Balzieland was the ancient name for the estate of Logan. It is not known when the original building was built, but it is believed to have been the McDouall of Logan family stronghold from the 13th century. About the year 1500 the old house of Balzieland was accidentally destroyed by fire, causing the loss of the old family papers of Patrick M'Douall of Logan. It was then rebuilt as a tower house. Its remains can be seen in the 30-acre Logan Botanic Garden, which was constructed upon the old castle gardens under the influence of Agnes Buchan-Hepburn of Smeaton, who married James McDouall in 1869.

Fergus D. H. Macdowall

Logan House on the grounds of the Logan Botanic Garden

Location—In the Parish of Kirkmaiden in Wigtonshire. Situated in the northwest of the 30-acre Logan Botanic Garden, 14 miles south of Stranraer and 1½ miles north of Port Logan, in the South Rhinns of Galloway.

Description—There are some remains of a 16ᵗʰ century tower house in the Logan Botanic Garden at Logan House. An ivy-covered fragment of the south angle of the old castle has been incorporated into the garden wall on the northwest of the Botanic Garden. This wall fragment is 12 feet long, 3½ feet thick and rises 30 feet high. It contains the remains of a ground floor vault and window jambs from the 1ˢᵗ and 2ⁿᵈ floors of the old tower house.

Castle Semple

Origin—Castleton Castle (Castle Semple) was constructed between 1492 and 1550 on the site of a structure built in the 13ᵗʰ century at the east end of the loch at Lochwinnoch. Colonel William MacDowall, son of William McDowall 15ᵗʰ of Garthland, purchased Castleton and Eliotstoun, and the 900-acre Castle Semple walled property, and much of Renfrewshire beyond it from Hew the 11ᵗʰ Lord Semple in 1727. The ruinous castle was demolished to be replaced in 1735 by Castlesemple House, an elaborate mansion with extensive gardens designed by Robert Adam.

Col. William McDowall obtained an Act to make the lands of Castlesemple a feudal barony, perhaps the last of its kind. The third William MacDowall of Castlesemple, M.P. and of Garthland (Wigtownshire) and King's Lord Lieutenant of Renfrewshire, had plans made to rebuild Castlesemple House in the style of Culzean Castle of the Kennedy Marquess of Ailsa, Ayrshire. The plans are now in the British Museum, London. The estate included the now ruinous Collegiate Kirk of the Semples (Sempill, now) with the three generations of McDowalls buried under the aisle. The most anciently venerable object on the estate sits just outside the north walls. It is the Clochodrick Stone, a massive meteorite laden with once molten iron and inscribed with crosses and old Irish Ogham script to mark the burial place of King Ryderrich Hale of the Strathclyde Britons seated at Dumbarton Castle across the Clyde. Ryderrich's Christian Bishop was St. Mungo, a man of royal descent who founded Glasgow. As a boy he was a contemporary of King Arthur of Britain and later of King Aiden of the Dalriadic Scots as well as being a close friend and collaborator of Columcille (St. Columba) of Iona.

The Semples built a pele on an islet on Semple Loch on the estate, in which they later took refuge in Queen Mary's reign. Now ruinous and hidden in the Aird Meadow, it is a part of Muirshiel Park of the County of Renfrew, managed for the Macdowalls of Garthland estate by the Royal Society for the Protection of Birds.

The original seat of the present James Lord Sempill (Chief of that Name) is the ruin of the Eliotstoun Castle directly across the Black Cart water from their Castle Semple. Jamie was the Organizing Director of the "Gathering 2009" in Edinburgh in his role as Vice-Convener of The Standing Council of Scottish Chiefs of which Fergus D. H. Macdowall is a member.

Location—In the parish of Lochwinnoch in Renfrewshire. Its ruin is situated in Castle Semple Country Park, itself part of the Muirshiel Regional Park.

Description—Ruins such as the west gate remain at the south end of the loch. The mansion burned down in 1924. The ruined shell was destroyed by the County except for the billiard room and stable wings, which have been re-roofed and used as modern homes and as farm buildings.

From a postcard in Fergus D. H. Macdowall archive, by RDC Museums
Castlesemple House in 1907

Courtesy of Fergus D. H. Macdowall
Architectural Drawing of Castlesemple House

Cruggleton Castle

Origin—This was originally the site of an Iron Age fort located high on a rocky promontory above the sea. By 1014 the Scot "Earl" Malcolm, is believed to have lived at Cruggleton in a fortification rebuilt by him or by Norsemen who preceded him. Then the Lords of Galloway built a motte here with a bailey on the landward side. In the 1230s, Alan of Galloway (died 1234) or his daughter Elena built a wall 7 to 9 feet thick and 78 feet square around the top of the motte.

After the old Celtic Lords of Galloway, the castle passed in 1264 to the Comyns who expended ample revenues from their estates on it. The 12th century motte structure was followed by a castle in about 1260 that was further strengthened in the 1280s. Cruggleton was captured in 1282 by King Edward I of England during the Scottish Wars of Independence. In 1289 the castle, a residence of the John Comyn at the time, had at least 8 towers to be roofed with lead. In 1296 the Comyns lost the castle to King Edward I for demanding the restoration of King John Baliol. After his abdication, the Castles of Botel (Buittle), Wigtown, and Cruggleton were committed by King Edward I to the keeping of Henry de Percy of Northumberland to be English fortifications. The English held Cruggleton until 1313. About 1314 Bruce gave the old Galloway Lordships and the Comyn's castle of Cruggleton to Lord Soulis. Later, after he was forfeited of it for conspiracy, Cruggleton Castle passed to the monks of Whithorn.

A successor tower house was built in the west corner of the castle court in the 1370s by Archibald "the Grim" Douglas, but it was torn down about 1455 when the Black Douglases were suppressed by King James II. By the late 16th century, the castle had been rebuilt with another tower house and demolished for materials by the 1680s. After Peter Macdowall of Machermore disponed his recently acquired Cruggleton Castle and contiguous lands in 1606, his barony faded out. About 1605 James Kennedy, son of Sir John of Blairquhan, married Sheriff Agnew's daughter Jane. His father settled Cruggleton Castle upon the young couple to be their residence. In 1613 Sir John was denounced as rebel for seizing Alexander Myrtoun and imprisoning him in the castle's dungeon. In 1620 the castle was transferred to Agnew of Lochnaw. By 1684 it was described by Symson as "wholly demolished and ruinous." A Marquess of Bute, as heritor of the McDougall of Freugh lands in Galloway, made minor restorative repairs to the ruins.

Location—In the parish of Sorbie in Wigtownshire, 1½ miles south of Garlieston. Cruggleton Castle occupied a very strong site on the Machars of Dumfries and Galloway, on a promontory bounded by sea cliffs and far from any modern road. The ruins of an ancient chapel from the times of the Celtic church still exist ¼ mile from Cruggleton's ruin.

Description—This large castle was a strong seaside fortification perched high on a sea cliff overlooking Wigtown Bay. It now lies overgrown in a ruin. The castle was built on a rock 30 feet above the surrounding ground, with the summit defended by an enclosing wall. In 1289 the castle had at least 8 towers, which were probably wooden. Nothing remains but a fragment of 6 feet of barrel-vaulted apartment from the 1370s tower house at the south end of the site. On the west side was a semicircular ditch 36 feet wide and 7 feet deep where an earthen embankment enclosed a bailey. The entrance to the castle was a 13 feet wide causeway across the ditch. There is a motte in the southeast corner of the bailey standing 14 feet high.

Castle Freugh (Castle M'Dowall, Castle MacDougall)

Origin—The date it was built is not known. The proper spelling of the ancient name of the property would appear to be Freuch or Frewch, meaning "dry" as applied to corn (grain, not maize). In the 15th century the property belonged to M'Dowalls of Freugh. Castle Freugh latterly bore the name of Castle M'Dowall or Castle MacDougall, though it was actually a tower house. John McDouall, Laird of Freugh, was a high Royalist supporter of King Charles I. In 1654 the castle was attacked by enemy Cromwell's forces. John McDouall of Freugh escaped capture but his house "Balgreggan" and his fortalice "Castle MacDougall" were burnt with their records. By 1684 the Laird of Freugh had taken up residence at Balgreggan House. Symson in 1684 mentions that Balgreggan was then a good strong house and was the ordinary residence of the Laird of Freugh. The Freugh and Balgreggan estates have since been united for more than two centuries. Balgreggan House was demolished in 1966.

Location—In the parish of Stoneykirk in Wigtownshire. Located in the Rhinns of Galloway about 4 miles southeast of Stranraer and just west of Sandhead village. From what can be gathered, Castle Freugh stood close to the motte hill still preserved near the site of Balgreggan House.

Description—Nothing remains of the tower of Castle Freugh itself. Crop marks reveal a number of rectilinear enclosures in the field where the tower stood, close to the still preserved motte. The tower and its policies are depicted on J. Gillone's survey plan of 1795, but by 1847 the tower had been demolished and only a trace of the parkland was still visible. Near to it stood Balgreggan House, which was demolished in 1966.

Garthland Tower (Castle)

Origin—An early spelling of Macdowall of Garthland's first "seat" was "Gairachloyne" interpreted as "joyful tufted mount," but it was originally named "Caerlachlan" or "Fort of the Norse." In 1684 Symson wrote that the Garthland Tower was "a good old strong house." It was held by the Macdowalls of Garthland as their *caput baroniae* for six centuries, until the entire estate had to be sold for government debts in 1811 by William Macdowall 20th of Garthland and 3rd of Castlesemple. Soon the tower became the property of the Earls of Stair, and is to this day. In 1822 an observer wrote that "a cornerstone of the Castle bears the date 1211 and another stone (on the battlements towards the east) 1274." As late as 1839 it was recorded in the Parish Statistics as standing 45 feet high.

After the sale in 1811, the estates of Barr and Garpel in Renfrewshire became the substitute barony of Garthland with Garthland House. Professor Fergus Day Hort Macdowall matriculated at the Lyon Court in 1987 as the Laird and Baron of the Feudal Baronies of Garthland and Castlesemple, Chief of the Name and Arms of MacDowall. He retains the site of Garthland Castle with its cairn at Garthland Mains near Stranraer, Wigtownshire, Scotland, and also the substitute estate of Garthland with his seat of Barr Castle in Lochwinnoch Parish, Renfrewshire, Scotland.

Fergus D. H. Macdowall

Garthland Mains Farmhouse and Cairn at the site of Garthland Castle

Location—In the parish of Stoneykirk in Wigtownshire, at Garthland Mains, 4 miles south of Stranraer. The Garthland Tower House stood 135 feet northeast of Garthland farmhouse.

Fergus D. H. Macdowall

Garthland Mains Cairn

Description—Every vestige of the old square tower or castle of Garthland has disappeared. Its stones were taken as building materials for new farm houses and stone fences. The stone bearing the date 1274, although defaced, was built into the archway between two buildings at Garthland Mains farm. Three other stones which bear a roll molding probably came from the tower and were built into the external masonry of the farmstead, at the southeast angle. The date-stone was finally incorporated in a cairn erected on the site by Fergus D. H. Macdowall, circa 1980.

Heston Island

Origin—Heston Island was originally called Estholm by the Cistercian monks because it was the most easterly part of their Dundrennan Abbey lands when the abbey was founded by Fergus Lord of Galloway in 1142. Heston Island was the site of Sir Duncan Macdowyll's stronghold, which he held for the Baliol Kings from 1310 until 1353. This island location gave command of the nearby waters. In the documents of the time, the stronghold is referred to as a pele, which means that its tower likely stood within a defensive stockade. Duncan Macdowyll was a loyal supporter of his related patron King John Baliol and hostile to his opponent Robert the Bruce until the latter died in 1329. Duncan Macdowyll led Galloway in support of Scotland under David II and was captured with him. Then Duncan was obliged to help restore the Baliol monarchy.

The restored King Edward Baliol built a fortified manor house on Heston Island after obtaining land from the monks at Dundrennan Abbey. The house was completed in 1342 and was garrisoned by Duncan Macdowyll in support of the Baliol residence at nearby Botel castle until 1345, when King Edward Baliol fled to England. In 1345 the English attacked Heston Island, burned Macdowyll's pele, and took him prisoner again. In 1353 Sir Duncan Macdowyll's stronghold was conquered by the resurgent Scots under Sir William Douglas. Sir Duncan was escorted to the High Stewart to confirm his allegiance to King David II, who was still held captive in England.

Location—In the parish of Rerrick, Stewartry of Kirkcudbright, on Heston Island, a small island at the mouth of the river Urr. The island is about 7 miles south of Dalbeattie on minor roads.

Description—There are no visible ruins of Duncan Macdowyll's pele. Remains can still be seen of the fortified manor house built by King Edward Baliol in 1342. Baliol's manor house was 36 feet long and 15 feet wide, with walls 3 feet thick.

Kenmure Castle

Origin—Kenmure Castle was fortified as one of the seats of the Lords of Galloway. There is also a tradition that Dervorgilla rebuilt it. After her son King John I's downfall in 1296, the property passed to the Gordons of Lochinvar in 1297. This is the well-known Gordon family castle of the Viscounts Kenmure.

Location—In the parish of Kells in Kirkcudbrightshire. The ruin sits on a circular mount, 5/8 of a mile above the head of Loch Ken, and 3/4 mile southeast of New Galloway.

Description—Kenmure Castle is roofless and in a state of decay. The ruin occupies the flat summit of a lofty knoll. Traces of the moat are still visible on the west side.

Kirkcudbright Castle (Castlemains, Castledykes)

Origin—It started out as an earth-and-timber Royal Castle on Castlemains or Castledykes under the successive reigns of Kings Malcolm IV to Alexander III, then to John Baliol. Its defense was within the jurisdiction of the Lords of Galloway. Uchtred who was murdered in 1174 at his nearby Palace Isle would have stayed here also. In 1361 Fergus Macdowyll, third surviving son of Duncan of Heston Isle, was appointed to be Sheriff or Constable of this Kirkcudbright Castle with "ane three merk land" by royal charter from King David II. It was held by the Douglases from 1369 until their forfeiture to the crown in 1455. Castlemains then passed to the Scottish crown which in turn granted it to the Borough of Kirkcudbright in 1509.

Location—In the Parish of Kirkcudbright in the Stewartry of Kirkcudbright. This castle was west of the town of Kirkcudbright at the mouth of the Dee River at a place now called Castledykes where it commanded the entrance of the harbor. It is not to be confused with the later 16th century Maclellan castle in the town of Kirkcudbright itself.

Description—In old deeds, the lands are called Castle Mains, but now they bear the name Castledykes. The existing earthworks form a central mound, 196 by 80 feet, with an uneven surface. The castle mounds are surrounded by a deep ditch or fosse generally 30 feet deep, except near the east corner where the fosse is 20 feet deep. The tide probably flowed around the deep fosse to fill it with water. There are some traces of a bailey about 450 feet long, with ditches on each side, and a number of mounds suggesting the remains of ramparts.

Traces of the building are still apparent but there is no masonry extant and it has been long demolished.

Excavations from 1911 to 1913 revealed foundation courses nowhere more than 2½ feet high. The wall foundations were 9½ to 7½ feet thick and they enclosed an area about 95 by 55 feet. At each corner there were towers 36½ feet in diameter. The eastern tower formed one of the externally buttressed gate towers. The foundations of the southwest tower were 44 feet in diameter.

Kirkhill Mote (See also Abbey Church of Lincluden)

Origin—Fergus Lord of Galloway built an early 12th century earthwork bailey and motte fortress, now called Kirkhill Mote, just west of the banks of River Nith, 1 mile north of Dumfries. His son, Uchtred

Lord of Galloway, founded a Benedictine abbey church on the site of the bailey as a nunnery in 1164. It was suppressed in 1389 by Archibald "the Grim" Earl of Douglas, who replaced the nunnery with a college of secular canons. The domestic buildings were later fortified with further construction after the Reformation. This was called Lincluden College.

Location—In the parish of Terregles in Dumfriesshire, on the summit of a hill 1 mile north of Dumfries Town Center on the A780-A76 Route in Lincluden, off Abbey Lane. The site is owned by Historic Scotland.

Description—A mound 1 or 2 feet high and from 12 to 18 feet wide encloses a nearly circular space about 200 feet in diameter. Within it, at the south side, there is a flat-topped mound about 13 feet high and from 40 to 50 feet in diameter. Its top is pitted with small squarish depressions. The ground is slightly trenched, both outside and inside the enclosing mound. Adjacent are the stone ruins of the Lincluden College including a 16th century tower house built after the Reformation.

Longcastle (Longcaster)

Origin—Longcastle was first mentioned in 1330 when in the possession of a scion of the M'Dowalls of Garthland, who built a castle on an island in Dowalton Loch as fortification of an ancient crannog about that time. Later the lands of Longcastle were owned briefly by the McDoualls of Freugh. The "McDouall" spelling was adopted by Dowalton after they became McDoualls of Logan and, later still, Freugh followed suit. At one time Longcastle and Ravenstone were one large property, but later were divided. About 1445 it was listed as a possession of Gilbert M'Dowall styled of Ravenstone and Freugh but, by 1496, records show it as a possession of the Mures of Claichlaw, who sold it soon after. In the Survey of Timothy Pont in Blaeu's Atlas, Dowalton Loch was called the Loch of Boirlant. Longcastle was at the western shore of the former Dowalton Loch. At that time it was in the former Longcastle or Longcaster Parish, which was annexed to the adjacent Kirkinner Parish about 1650. Only ruins of a crumbling castle wall remained when the 132-acre loch was completely drained by three local landowners in the 1860s.

Location—Dowalton Loch was situated about 5 miles from Whithorn in the center of the Machars district in the parish of Kirkinner in Wigtownshire. Longcastle lies on Route A714, 6 miles south-southwest of Wigtown in marsh and scrub, some distance from any road. The area is now a nature reserve under the care of the Scottish Wildlife Trust.

Description—In 1911 the site of Longcastle was described as an artificial island composed of large blocks of stone. On the north side were the remains of an apparent castle wall 4½ feet thick.

There are visible remains of an enclosure surrounded by marsh. This enclosure measured 100 feet by 65 feet within the turf-covered footings of a stone wall up to 11 feet wide. The entrance probably lay on the north side.

Within the interior of the enclosure there were once two rectangular buildings around a central court, enclosed on the north side by a small curved wall. The longer building was on the south side. It had two partitions and measured 47 by 15½ feet internally within faced walls 2½ feet thick and up to 3 feet high. In a worse condition were the ruins of a smaller rectangular building 32 feet long by 14½ feet wide, with 2½ feet thick walls and divided by a partition wall 2 feet thick.

Machermore Castle

Origin—The plain of arable land in the center of Galloway is called "Machermore," meaning "the great level plain." The castle dates to the 11th century and perhaps earlier.

After defeating the Macdowalls and their allies, Robert the Bruce is said to have gifted the lands of Machermore and Kirroughtree to Peter M'Lurg, a local man who loyally followed him, with his two brothers. In the 16th century Machermore's old square tower was the seat of Macdowall of Machermore (Machrimore). After Peter Macdowall of Machermore disponed his recently acquired Cruggleton Castle and contiguous lands in 1606, his

Fergus D. H. Macdowall
Machermore Castle as a modern-day seniors' home

Machermore barony faded out. In 1682 Graham of Claverhouse made Machermore Castle a lookout post and a base for troops seeking out Covenanters. Machermore Castle changed hands until it came into a long period of ownership by the Dunbar family.

Location—In Minnigaff Parish, west Kirkcudbrightshire, situated near the east bank of the Cree River, approximately 1½ miles southeast of Newton Stewart. It lies just off the A75 Euroroute.

Description—This well-preserved old castle is now the stately and modern Machermore Castle Care Home. There is tradition set to rhyme that says a kettle full of gold is buried under a flat rock somewhere around Machermore Castle:

> Between the castle and the River Cree
> lies enough o' gold to set a' Scotland free.

Tower of Mindork

Origin—The build date of the tower is not known, but in the 15th century the MacDowalls of Mindork were on record as a cadet of the Macdowalls of Garthland. In 1494 Uchtred M'Dowall of Dalregill, Uchtred M'Dowall of Mundork, and others were required to return livestock and property, and to pay costs to the sheriff for having participated in an illegal raid upon his lands. In 1528 during a feud with the Hamiltons that began the year before, the Macdowalls of Freuch and the Macdowalls of Mindork invaded the Isle of Arran and burned Brodick Castle to the ground. In September 1638, Mindork Tower was held by Uchtred M'Dowall of Mundork, no doubt a son of Uchtred and Lady Catherine Herries. This Uchtred was the last of the M'Dowalls of Mondork. In the following generation, Mindork passed to the Stewarts of Garlies. M'Kerlie related a disputed story about Uchtred's fate:

> In 1830, a Captain Robert M'Kerlie obtained an account of the last possessor of the tower from James Hannah, the venerable tenant of the farm, then in his eightieth year. He stated that the last laird became indebted to the Crown in certain duties (more probably fines) which he was unable to pay. The Stewarts, with or without authority, harassed him, with the ultimate view of obtaining the property. For safety, the laird went into hiding at the Spittal of Bladenoch, trusting to a friend, who, however, betrayed him. The laird was seized and barbarously used, even to having his beard set on fire and entirely consumed. He was then taken to Wigton, and locked up in the jail, where he died. The body, not being interred, was allowed to waste away.

Location—In the parish of Kirkcowan in Wigtownshire, about 1½ miles southwest of Kirkcowan, on minor roads south of Route B733, and 1 mile east of High Mindork. The tower was situated on the farm of Lower Mindork on the southwest side of the old Glenluce road.

Description—At the site is a pile of stones of the old residence on a hillock 230 feet in height. From the site, the tower appears to have been small, square, and contracted. By local tradition, two rows of outhouses formed the approach to the entrance and the tower had beautifully cut stone at the corners and windows. A solitary ash tree marked the remains of the Tower of Mindork at the end of the 18th century and may still do so.

Mote of Urr

Origin—This mound site itself may date back to ancient times. The Mote of Urr was built as a Norman-style motte by Fergus Lord of Galloway in precaution against King David I of the Royal Castle of Dumfries sometime between 1130 and 1160, then was destroyed in 1174. When rebuilt as a timber tower surrounded by palisade fortifications, the Mote of Urr was built 6 feet higher than before. There is little trace of occupation after the early 1300s. A Burgh of Urr existed by 1262, but soon after disappeared. The nearby Buittle Castle was probably the natural successor to this fortification for the defense of Western Galloway.

Location—In the parish of Urr in Wigtownshire. It stood half a mile upstream from Buittle Castle and one mile northwest of Dalbeattie, in the valley of the Urr Water, on the banks of the river.

Description—This ancient mound site covers 5½ acres. The Mote of Urr had a central tower of timber, but no sign of it remains now. The heavy timber palisade was reinforced with rough stone and probably had turrets abutting on its inner surface. Traces of the ancient rampart and ditch can still be seen. The motte rises 35 feet above a deep ditch surrounding it. A well preserved oval bailey that measured 450 × 240 feet then entirely surrounds this motte and ditch.

Palace Isle in Lochfergus

Origin—Sometime between the years 1138 and 1140, Fergus Lord of Galloway built Palace Isle as his principal seat. It was at the center of an island called Palace Isle in a loch called Lochfergus. It was said to be the favorite home of his wife, the Princess Elizabeth of England. The loch contained three islands, partly natural and partly manmade. The northernmost is called Palace Isle and the smaller southernmost is called Rough Isle or Stable Isle. The middle isle seems to be unnamed.

Fergus' son Uchtred lived here and at nearby Kirkcudbright Castle (Castlemains). It was here that on 22 September 1174, Uchtred's nephew Malcolm captured and fatally mutilated him. In 1471, the lands of Lochfergus passed by charter to the Maclellans of Bomby—a former Macdowall estate. On 25 February 1498 at Lochfergus, the palace of the old Lords of Galloway, then belonging to the powerful Laird of Bomby, was destroyed with fire by John Carnys in the Copwood, Thon Hutchenson, and others to whom King James IV afterwards granted remission for the deed. The ruined walls remained standing till about the year 1570, when Maclellan of Bomby used their stones for his Kirkcudbright Castle.

Location—In the parish of Kirkcudbright in the Stewartry of Kirkcudbright, 2 miles east of Kirkcudbright, uphill on the north side of the Route B727, on the farm of Lochfergus.

Description—Lochfergus is now drained and no ruins of the castle are visible. Palace Isle was about 390 feet in diameter. The castle was an oblong building surrounded by a wall with towers placed at each of its four corners in the Norman fashion. The south end of Palace Isle seems to have been cut by a moat or ditch to divide the castle from its courtyard. There is now no trace of a castle or buildings on Palace Isle.

On Stable Isle there is an oval, tree-covered hillock 12 to 14 feet high. At Stable Isle's south end are traces of a rampart about 4 feet high and an oblong building 45 × 18 feet. The *Ordnance Survey Object Name Book* states that Stable Isle was fortified and covered with wood. At Stable Isle's center is the ruin or site of a house about 25 × 16 feet— probably the stable pertaining to Castle Fergus.

Abbeys of the Lords of Galloway

*Scott A. MacDougald, Walter M. Macdougall,
and Fergus D. H. Macdowall*

Dundrennan Abbey

Origin—The name *Dun-nan-droigheann* means "fort of the thorn-bushes." Dundrennan was founded in 1142 as a Cistercian Monastery by Fergus Lord of Galloway. This abbey of Cistercian monks was formed as a daughter house of Rievaulx Abbey in Yorkshire. The initial building work would have taken fifty years or more. The abbey lands once reached as far east as Heston Island, then called Estholm. Dundrennan, in turn, became the motherhouse of Glenluce and Sweetheart Abbeys.

In the 14th century the abbey underwent reconstruction, which may well be due to damages incurred during the Wars of Independence. After these wars the Cistercians made claims against both Edward I and Edward III to obtain compensation for acts of their English armies.

After losing the battle of Langside in May 1568, Mary Queen of Scots spent her last night in Scotland at Dundrennan before embarking for England in a fishing boat from Port Mary, 2 miles south of the abbey. Reconstruction and layout changes continued until circa 1590, but from about 1630–1850 there was major robbing of stone from buildings within the abbey for use in other structures, such as the manse property. The abbey estate now belongs to the family of Maitland of Dundrennan.

Location—The abbey ruins are in the parish of Rerrick in Kirkcudbrightshire, about 4½ miles southeast of Kirkcudbright, near the village of Dundrennan. The abbey is a little over 1 mile inland and has a view of the Firth of Solway.

Description—Architecturally it is a fine example of the Early Pointed style, but only the transept and choir remain. The tomb of Alan Lord of Galloway (died 1234) is on the east side of the north transept in a wall niche formed by a Norman arch with a single round filleted molding. His damaged effigy, the "Belted Knight," shows chain armour at the neck, armpits, knees, and head. One belt, buckled in front, encircles the waist, and a second passes over the right shoulder. The right hand seems to have held a sword. His lady is said to have been buried in a niche on the west side.

Sheila McDowell

Sheila McDowell

Sheila McDowell

Dundrennan Abbey

Glenluce Abbey

Origin—Glenluce was founded about 1192 as a daughter-house of the Cistercian monks of Dundrennan Abbey by Roland 3rd Lord of Galloway (died 1200), the older brother of Duegald. Glenluce Abbey survived the other abbeys by a century, but fell into ruin after the Reformation. The abbey was secularized in 1602 upon the death of the last monk. Circa 1600, Thomas Hay of Park and his wife Janet (Margaret), daughter of John Macdowall 12th of Garthland, used its stones to largely build Park Castle (now available to rent).

Location—In the parish of Old Luce, 2 miles northwest of the village of Glenluce in Wigtownshire. The ruins are in a site of great natural beauty on the Water of Luce.

Description—The ruins comprise a fragment of the south transept wall of the abbey church as well as outbuildings. The water supply is a unique survival. Earthenware pipes, jointed and with inspection chambers, lie in their original positions, exposed to view.

The fine chapterhouse of late 15th or 16th century date is the best preserved building and is complete, but the remainder of the ruin seldom stands above the foundation level. On the ceiling in the chapterhouse is carved the crowned lion rampant in the arms of Galloway. These are the arms of Fergus Lord of Galloway's successive heirs, including the Abbey's founder, Roland, and the Macdowalls of Garthland. The site is cared for by Historic Scotland.

Sheila McDowell

**Galloway/Garthland Macdowall arms on the
ceiling of the Glenluce Chapterhouse**

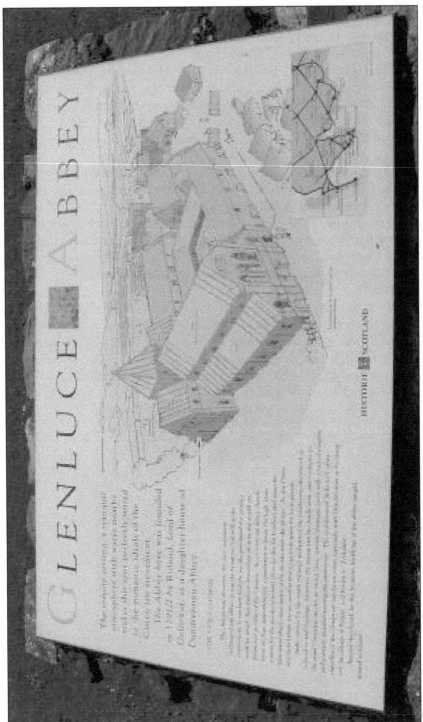

Sheila McDowell

Sheila McDowell

Glenluce Abbey

Lincluden Abbey

Origin—Uchtred Lord of Galloway (died 1173) founded a Benedictine nunnery circa 1161–65 on the site of the bailey of Kirkhill Mote near Dumfries. It was suppressed in 1389 by Archibald "the Grim" Earl of Douglas, with Papal permission. Archibald the Grim replaced the original nunnery with a college of secular canons, whose domestic buildings were fortified with further construction after the Reformation.

Location—On a hill summit 1 mile north of Dumfries Town Center on the A780-A76 Route in Lincluden. It lies on a bend of the Cluden Water near where it joins the River Nith.

Description—After it was abandoned in 1700, the site was used a stone quarry until protected in 1882. Now the ruin is cared for by Historic Scotland.

Saulseat Abbey (Soulseat Abbey)

Origin—This was the first abbey founded by Fergus Lord of Galloway. Circa 1160 he handed it over to the Premonstratensian Order of Monks from Premontre in Picardy. The abbey sat on the promontory of a loch with a very narrow isthmus.

Location—In the parish of Inch, in Wigtownshire, 2 miles east of Stanraer on Route A757, on Soulseat Loch near the ruins of Castle Kennedy.

Description—The west tower of the abbey still stood in 1684 at the time Symson wrote his description of Galloway, but now only one reminiscent stone survives nearby behind the manse built in 1838. The site is now the Meadowsweet Herb Garden, and it is open to the public in the summer months.

Sweetheart Abbey (New Abbey)

Origin—Founded by Dervorgilla Lady of Galloway, as a Cistercian Abbey in 1273, in memory of her husband John Baliol (died 1269). Baliol is the old Scots spelling and Balliol was the Norman/English spelling of the name. Dervorgilla is buried in the sanctuary of the abbey church, along with a casket containing her beloved husband's embalmed heart. The monks called the abbey *Dulce Cur* ("Sweetheart") in honor of this. In the late 1300s the abbey came under the protection of Archibald "the Grim" Earl of Douglas.

Location—The abbey's substantial remains are 5 miles south of Dumfries, on the east side of the village of New Abbey.

Description—After 1608 many of the stones of the abbey were robbed to be reused as building materials in the nearby village of New Abbey, but in 1779 early preservation efforts saved the shell of the church as well as some other parts from complete destruction. The site is cared for by Historic Scotland.

Priory of St. Mary's Isle (Priory St. Maria de Trayle)

Origin—In 1161, to show his penitence for rebelling against David I King of Scots, Fergus Lord of Galloway built the Priory St. Maria de Trayle on an isle once called the Isle of Trahyl. It was a magnificent monastery dedicated to the Virgin Mary. The Augustinian Priory on St. Mary's Isle was first mentioned in a charter of 1189. Later the Priory was united as a cell of Holyrood Abbey. It was virtually independent by 1511 or 1512, but was becoming ruinous by then. The priory lands were finally granted to James Lidderdale and his son in 1608.

Location—In the parish of Kirkcudbright, on Route A711 south of the town of Kirkcudbright.

Description—The site of St. Maria de Trayle is now called St. Mary's Isle, but the isle has become a peninsula. The priory site is now covered by coniferous trees. No remains of the priory are visible.

The Priory St. Maria de Trayle was surrounded by high walls, with two entrance gates to it. The outer gate is called the Great Cross, located about ½ mile from the inner gate. Little Cross is the name of the inner east gate leading to the cells inhabited by the monks. Centuries later the seat of the Earl of Selkirk was situated on St. Mary's Isle. At this house Robert Burns gave the famous Selkirk grace. It was also here that the American sea captain John Paul Jones landed in 1778, in a failed attempt to kidnap the Earl of Selkirk to exchange for American prisoners. In the earl's absence, Jones took the silver plate, which he later returned to Lady Selkirk.

Tongland Abbey

Origin—The parish of Tongland belonged anciently to the monks of Iona, of the Scottish-Irish Church that was forfeited to Rome by King David I. The name derived from the Norwegian or Danish word *tunga*, "a strip of land," since the church was on a tongue of land between the rivers Dee and Tarf. Fergus Lord of Galloway may have built a church here as early as 1161, only two miles upstream from his home on Palace Isle.

The Premonstratensian Abbey of Tongland was founded in 1218, probably by Alan of Galloway, and colonized by monks who came from Cockersand Abbey in Lancashire. It appears that the whole of Tongland Parish belonged to the abbey, and it rented the lands to tenants.

In 1296 the Abbot Alexander swore fealty to King Edward I, likely in support of John Baliol's claim to the throne of Scotland. In 1325 local Gallowegians slew the abbot and his sacrist inside the church because they were foreigners who had sworn allegiance to Edward I. Afterwards they had to appear before the King with halters round their necks to receive their sentences. In 1530 the abbey was united with the Bishopric of Galloway at the request of King James V, to improve the abbey's standards. In the 1600s the western transept of the abbey was adapted to create a parish church, whose ruins now sit upon the abbey ruins.

Location—In the parish of Tongland, 2 miles northeast of the town of Kircudbright, in the Village of Tongland on Route A711. The abbey ruins sit between the vacated Tongland Parish Church and the grounds of Mansewood House.

Description—The materials of Tongland Abbey were used in building the manse, the cornmill, a former papermill, the old bridge, and some of the local houses. In the 1600s, abbey remains were also incorporated into the now derelict Tongland Parish Church. Only part of the abbey's north wall and the west gable remain. The north wall is now 28 feet long and 9 feet high. The west gable is at its original height of 19 feet and is surmounted by a square stone belfry. Inside are several carved stone fragments of earlier windows.

The last abbot of Tongland Abbey was appointed in 1504, in the reign of James IV. He was an Italian alchemist named Damian, who tried to fly to France from the wall of Stirling Castle but instead fell into a midden and fractured his thigh bone. He attributed his fall to his wings having been made by blending cock's feathers with eagle's feathers—he claimed he fell because cocks naturally prefer to be on the ground.

Mary Queen of Scots rested at Tongland Abbey in her flight from her defeat at the Battle of Langside on 13 May 1568.

Tongland Abbey's Bishop's Palace and Palace Yard

Origin—Tongland Abbey and its estates persisted as a regality of its abbots and bishops in the Bishopric of Galloway until the abbey was abolished in 1689. These bishops undoubtedly had their own bishop's palace with its palace yard, but only a part of a wall remains now. Such residences were lightly fortified, to deter marauders. In August 1300 when King Edward I advanced from Kirkcudbright to Cally and sojourned at Enrick, he used Palace Yard as a place to hold his law courts. From this place he sent detachments into Wigtownshire, receiving support from the Baliol kinsman Sir Dougal MacDougall/MacDowyl of Gairochloyne, the native representative of the House of ancient Galloway and Chief of his Name there. Later the stones of the monastery were used to build the bridge over the Dee River.

Location—In the parish of Girthon in southwest Kirkcudbrightshire, at Enrick (or Enrig) near Gatehouse of Fleet, 9 miles west-northwest of Kirkcudbright. The site is south of Enrick and north of Route A75, on the west side of Route B727.

Description—The site is an oval plateau of earth in a low-lying meadow, measuring 352 feet by 194 feet. It was surrounded by a broad wet ditch about 50 feet wide and 6 or 7 feet deep when measured in 1911. The entrance was probably on the east side at a break in the ditch. The plateau level rises gradually from the lower west end until it is some 7 feet higher. About 70 feet from the east end of the plateau, there are indefinite foundations of a large rectangular building. No buildings remain, although there are marks surrounded by a fosse.

The *New Statistical Account of 1845* stated that some old plane trees were growing then, with a foliage different from those propagated at that time. Some of these venerable trees were still called the "Palace trees." Apparently the Palace was surrounded by a ditch and wall, and one of the arched gates was still standing within then living memory.

Whithorn Priory

Origin—Whithorn was founded by Fergus Lord of Galloway circa 1150 on a holy site as a cathedral of the Bishop of Whithorn, to replace St. Ninian's original church. It became a Priory by 1177 for the Premonstratensian Order of White Canons and was added to over the next 300 years.

Location—Just west of the main street in the town of Whithorn in Wigtownshire, on the peninsula between Luce and Wigtown Bays.

Description—The Protestant Reformation in 1560 caused the site to fall into disrepair. The end of the Bishops of Galloway in the 1600s led to the demise of the priory. The nave of the cathedral was then used as a parish church. The rest of the site crumbled and the main tower collapsed in the early 1700s. Some fragments of this priory still remain, notably the beautiful south door of late Norman work and the crypt from the southeast end of the 1100s cathedral. The nearby excavated Candida Casa was founded at Whithorn circa 397 by Saint Ninian, Scotland's first saint. The site is cared for by Historic Scotland.

Names and Spellings
Connected to MacDowall

Coyle	MacDouyl
Dole	M'Douwille
Dougal(l)	Macduoel
Doyle	Mcdoual
Dow	Mcdoll
Dowdle	M(a)cDowal(l)
Dowall	M(a)cDowell
Dowell	MacDowile
Dowler	MacDowilt
Dowling	MacDu(a)el
Dugle	McDuhile
Duvall	MacDull
Duwall	Macdu(u)yl
Kyle	Makdougall
MacDewell	Makdull
MacDill	Mcduwell
MacDole	M'Gowall
MacDool	Mactheuel
M(a)cDougal(l)	

Bibliography

Ancient History of the MacDowalls
Troubled Years
Struggles
Makdougals of Makerstoun
Macdowall/M'dowall of Stodrig
MacDougall/Macdowall of Lodvica, Duwall,
and von Wahl

Agnew, Sir Andrew, *A History of the Hereditary Sheriffs of Galloway*, Adam & Charles Black, Edinburgh, 1864.

Biddulph, Lady Mary, *Correspondence*, Makerstoun, Scotland, 2004.

Burke's Landed Gentry of Great Britain, The Kingdom of Scotland, 19th ed., vol. 1, 1981.

Crawford, George, Macdowall of Garthland, *The unpublished Garthland "Greenbook" MSS*, ca. 1738.

Elgenstierna, *Adliga ätten DUWALL*, nr 241 in Svenska adelus attartavlor, p. 355.

Elliot, Grace A., F.S.M.C., *Berwickshire Naturalists' Club Histories*, part 2, vol. 34.

Ewan, Elspeth, Editor, *Ancrum & Longnewton*, Borders Family History Society, Galashiels, Scotland, 1993.

Ewan, Elspeth, Editor, *Makerstoun*, Borders Family History Society, Galashiels, Scotland, 1993.

Hogarth, Reverend David, *Statistical Account of Scotland, Parish of Makerstoun*, November 1834.

Houston, R. A., *Scottish Literacy and the Scottish Identity*, Cambridge University Press, Cambridge, England, 1985.

Innes, Sir Thomas of Learney, 1956, Scots Heraldry, Oliver & Boyd, Edinburgh.

Lever, Tresham, *Lessudden House: Sir Walter Scott and the Scotts of Raeburn*, The Boydell Press, London, 1971.

Lockhart, J. G., *The Life of Scott*, Centenary Edition published by Adam & Charles Black, Edinburgh, 1872.

Macdougal-Hay, Anna-Maria, of Mackerstoun, *Hay-Macdougal of Mackerstoun, Burke's Commoners VIII, A Geneologcal and Heraldic History of the Commoners of Great Britain and Ireland*, London, ca. 1830.

Macdowall of Garthland, in *Burke's Landed Gentry*, vol. 3, Burke's Peerage Ltd., London, 1972.

Macdowall, Fergus D. H., *The Macdowalls of Galloway*, Fergus Macdowall of Garthland, 1985.

Macdowall, Fergus D. H., *The Macdowalls of Galloway*, in *The Tartan*, vol. 1, ed. 11, 12, 13, Clan MacDougall Society of North America, Inc., 1983.

MacKenzie, Rev. William, *The History of Galloway*, John Nicholson, Kirkcudbright, 1841.

Maxwell, Sir Herbert, *Dumfries and Galloway*, Wm. Blackwood & Sons, Edinburgh, 1896.

Maxwell, Sir Herbert, *A History of the House of Douglas*, vol. 1, Freemantle & Co., London, 1902.

McDouall of Logan, in *Burke's Landed Gentry*, Harrison & Sons, London, 1914.

McDowall, Michael G., *The Copper Inheritance: A History of the Kindred of McDowall of Scotland*, Oakleaf Works, Edinburgh, 2001.

McDowall, William, *History of the Burgh of Dumfries*, Adam & Charles Black, Edinburgh, 1867.

M'Kerlie, P. H., *History of the Lands and their Owners in Galloway*, vol. 1–4, Wm. Patterson, Edinburgh, 1877.

Moffat, Alistair, *The Borders*, Deerpark Press, Selkirk, 2002.

Nisbet, Alexander, *Heraldry*, vol. 1 and 2, Edinburgh, 1722.

Nisbet, Alexander, *A System of Heraldry*, vol. 1–3, Edinburgh, 1816.

Omand, Donald, ed., *The Borders Book*, Birlinn Limited, Edinburgh, 1995.

Pearson, Hesketh, *Sir Walter Scott, His life and Personality*, Harper & Brothers Publishers, New York, 1954.

Prebble, John, *The Lion in the North*, Penguin Books, New York, 1973.

Scott, Sir Walter, *Redgauntlet*, Oxford World's Classics, Oxford, Edition 1985.

Von Wahl, Ena v. Harpe and Dieter v. Wahl, *Erlebtes Livland die Familie v. Wahl, 1795–1993*, Anton H. Konrad Verlag, 1995.

Westward Exodus
Settlement in Early Colonial America
To Virginia and the Carolinas: The Great Wagon Road
Toward Revolution

Abernathy, Thomas P., *From Frontier to Plantation in Tennessee*.

Adams, Margaret Bickel, assorted articles, letters, and genealogies of McDowell-related families.

Adams, Margaret Bickel, *Family Connections Along the Blue Ridge: The Ancestry and Close Descendants of Margaret Erwin McDowell and James Thomas Walton*, Worldcomm, 1995.

Bain, Robert, *The Clans and Tartans of Scotland*, Collins, Glasgow & London.

Black, George F., *The Surnames of Scotland*, repr. 1965.

Boyer, Carl, *Ship Passenger Lists, The South (1538–1825)*, 3rd ed., CA, 1979.

Brown, Margie G., *General Abstracts, Revolutionary War Veterans Scrip Act 1852*.

Buchanan, John, *The Road to Guilford Courthouse: The American Revolution in the Carolinas*, John Wiley & Sons, Inc., New York, 1997.

Cartmell, Thomas K., *A History of Frederick County, Virginia*.

Cartmell, Thomas K., *Shenandoah Valley Pioneers and their Descendants – Berryville VA*, Virginia Book Co., 1899, repr. 1963.

Chalkley, Lyman, *Chronicles of the Scotch-Irish Settlement in Virginia: extracted from the original court records of Augusta County 1745–1800*, three volumes.

Collins: *The Clans of Scotland*.

Connelly, Ann McDowell Abernethy, assorted articles, letters, and genealogies of McDowell-related families.

DAR National Records, *The 100 Volumes*.

Dinsmore, John Walker, *The Scotch-Irish in America*, Chicago.

Dorman, John Frederick, compiler, *Orange County, Virginia Deeds Books 3 & 4, 1738-1741 (abstracts)*.

Draper, Lyman C., *King's Mountain and Its Heroes*, Cincinnati, 1881.

Draper, Lyman C., assorted letters w/Rev. John McDowell of Macon Co., NC.

Dunaway, Wayland F., *The Scotch-Irish of Colonial Pennsylvania*, Univ. of NC Press, 1944.

Dunlop, Lily D., *History of the McDowells of Mecklenburg, County, NC*, 1929.

Dunlop, Lily D., *History of Burke County*, 1981.

Durning, William and Mary, *Scotch-Irish Settlements in Northern Ireland 1610–1750*, 1992.

Eaton, Clement, *A History of the Old South.*

Egle, William Henry, *Pennsylvania Historical Society Working Papers.*

Ellsberry, Elizabeth Prather, *Marriage Records of Lincoln County, Kentucky.*

Ernst, Charmaine, *McPeters/McPheeters Family Genealogy.*

Ervin, Sara Sullivan, *South Carolinians in the Revolution.*

Ervin, Eunice, *Under the Forest Floor*, 1997.

Fouts, Raymond Park, *Marriages of Bertie County, North Carolina 1762–1868.*

Gilreath, Amelia C., compiler, *Frederick County, Virginia Deed Book Series*, vol. 1.

Greater Rappahanock Central Library Archives, Fredericksburg, Spotsylvania Co., VA.

Green, Thomas Marshall, *Historic Families of Kentucky*, 1889.

Greenlee, Ralph Stevens, *Greenlee Families.*

Handley Regional Library Archives, Winchester, Frederick Co., VA.

Harrison, J. Houston, *Settlers by the Long Grey Trail*, Baltimore, 1984.

Holcomb, Brent H., *Abstracts of Wills & Estates 1749–1795.*

Holcomb, Brent H. and Parker, Elmer O., *Mecklenburg County, North Carolina Deed Abstracts 1763–1779.*

Macdowall of Garthland, Fergus D. H., *The MacDowalls of Galloway: A Journal for Historical Research.*

MacDowell, Dorothy Kelly, *McDowells in America, a Genealogy*, Gateway Press.

MacDowell, Dorothy Kelly, *McDowells in America, a Genealogy, Supplement I*, Gateway Press.

McDowell, Jack D., *McDowells in America*, Dorothy Kelly McDowall, Supplement.

McDowell, John Hugh, *McDowells, Erwins/Irvins, and Connections*, C.B. Johnson & Co., Memphis, TN., 1918.

McDowell, Leo B., *Older than the Sun: My McDowell Family, A Historical Narrative.* (unpublished).

McDowell, Leo B., *Thistles, Shamrocks, and Magnolias*, (unpublished).

McDowell, Margaret Erwin, assorted articles on the McDowell and related families.

McDowell, Mary Kyle, *The McDowell Genealogy.*

McDowell, Mrs. James L., *McDowells in America*, Dorothy Kelly McDowall, Supplement.

McDowell, William J., *The Irish Connection.*

M'Kerlie, P. H., *History of the Lands and Their Owners in Galloway*, 1906 (Reprint).

McLean, William, *Highland Clans.*

Morton, Oren F., *The History of Augusta County*, Virginia.

Morton, Oren F., *A History of Rockbridge County*, VA., pt. 1 & pt. 2.

Norris, J. E., *History of the Lower Shenandoah Valley*, 1890.

O'Dell, Cecil, *Pioneers of Old Frederick County*, Virginia, 1995.

O'Brien, Michael J., *Irish Settlers in America*, vol. 1 & 2.

Powell, William S., ed. *Dictionary of North Carolina Biography*, vol. 4.

Quarles, Garland Redd, *Some Worthy Lives* – Stephens City, VA.

Quarles, Garland Redd, *Some Old Homes in Frederick County*, Virginia, 1990.

Ramsey, Robert W., *Carolina Cradle*. Univ. of NC Press, 1964.

Russell, George E., ed., *National Genealogical Society Quarterly*, vol. 71, 1983.

Rutley, Angela, from a collection of articles for the Augusta and Rockbridge
    Genealogical Society.

Sampson, Mrs. John R., *Kith and Kin*.

Semple, Mary, letters and genealogies of the McDowells, Irvines, Lyles, etc.

Sharf, J. Thomas, *History of Western Maryland*.

Shelton, James K., *Sheltons, McDowells, Walls, and related families*.

Simkins, Francis Butler & Roland, Charles Pierce, *A History of the South*.

The Burke County Historical Society, *The Heritage of Burke County*, 1981.

Tyler, Lyon Gardiner, ed., *Encyclopedia of Virginia Biography*, vol. 2, New York, 1915.

Unknown: *Cecil Judgements, S. K. Nov. 4 (1730–1732)*.

Unknown: *Chapel Hill*, Univ. of NC Press, 1964.

Unknown: *Americans of Gentle Birth and Their Ancestors*.

Various: *The Journal of the Virginia Genealogical Society*.

Various: *A History of Rockbridge County, Family Sketches and Biographical
    Paragraphs*.

Various: *Records of the Royal Assembly at New Bern, North Carolina (1750)*.

Various: *History of Rutherford & Burke County North Carolina*, vol. 1.

Various: Anson Co., NC Deed Extracts, 1749–1795.

Various: Anson Co., NC Early Wills.

Various: Burke Co., NC Deed Extracts.

Various: Buncombe Co., NC Deed Extracts.

Various: Burke Co., NC Early Wills.

Various: Haywood Co., NC Deed Extracts.

Waddell, Joseph A., *Annals of Augusta County 1726–1871*.

Wayland, John W., *25 Chapters on the Shenandoah Valley*.

Whitson, Dorothy Wilson, *An American Family and the Making of a Nation*.

Williams, T. J. C., *History of Frederick County, Maryland*.

Williams, T. J. C., *History of Lancaster County, Pennsylvania*.

Wulfeck, Dorothy Ford, *Marriages of Some Virginia Residents 1607–1800*.

McDowells of Virginia and Kentucky

Clark, Tomas D., and Kirkpatrick, Lee, *Exploring Kentucky*, New York, American Book
    Company, 1955.

Diehl, George West, *Rockbridge County, Virginia Notebook, Utica, Kentucky*, McDowell
    Publications, 1982.

Fischer, David Hackett, *Albions' Seed: Four British Folkways in America*, New
    York, Oxford University Press, 1989.

Green, Thomas Marshall, *Historic Families of Kentucky with Special Reference to Stocks
    Immediately Derived from the Valley of Virginia*, Baltimore, Genealogical
    Publishing Company, 1975.

Harrison, J. Houston, *Settlers by the Long Grey Trail: Some Pioneers to Old Augusta
    County, Virginia, and Their Descendents of the Family of Harrison and Allied
    Lines*, Baltimore, Genealogical Publishing Company, 1975.

Internet: Henderson, Archibald, *The Conquest of the Old Southwest*.

Internet: McDowell, Leo B., *My McDowell Family*, 2000.

Kegley, F. B., *Kegley's Virginia Frontier: the Beginnings of the Southwest, the Roanoke
    of Colonial Days*, Roanoke, Virginia, Southwest Virginia Historical Society,
    1938.

Kennedy, Billy, *The Scots-Irish In The Shenandoah Valley*, Causeway Press, Londonderry, 1996.

MacDowell, Dorothy Kelly, *McDowells in America: a Genealogy*, Baltimore, Gateway Press, 1981.

McDowall, J. Kevan, *Carrick-Gallovidian*, Ayr, Scotland, Homer McCririck, 1947.

McDowell, John Hugh, *History of the McDowells and Connections*, C. B. Johnston, 1918.

Morton, Oren, *A History of Highland County*, Baltimore, Regional Publishing Company, 1979.

Morton, Oren F., *A History of Rockbridge County,* Baltimore, Regional Publishing Company, 1980.

Niles, Blair, *The James: from Iron Gate to the Sea*, New York, Rinehart, 1945.

Peyton, J. Lewis, *History of Augusta County, Staunton, Virginia*, S. M. Yost and Son, 1882.

Wayland, John W., *Historic Homes of Northern Virginia and the Eastern Panhandle of West Virginia*, Staunton, Virginia, The McClure Company, Inc. 1937.

MacDowalls in the U.S. Civil War

Burke County Historical Society, *The Heritage of Burke County*, 1981.

Catton, Bruce, *Terrible Swift Sword*, Doubleday, New York, 1963.

Connelly, Ann McDowell Abernethy, assorted articles, letters, and genealogies of McDowell-related families.

Ervin, Eunice, *Under the Forest Floor*, 1997.

Highland Historical Society, *Highland County and the Civil War*, McDowell, Virginia, 2005.

Letters of Robert Irwin McDowell, Rebecca Brevard McDowell, and Mary Anna Jackson, *VMI Archives Collection.*

National Park Service, *CWSAC Battle Summaries*, Internet, 2008.

Sifakis, Stewart, *Who Was Who in the Civil War, Volume 1, Facts on File*, New York, 1988.

Wise, Jennings C., *The Military History of VMI.*

Wise, John S., *An End of an Era.*

Thain MacDowell: Hero

Bishop, Arthur, *Legion Magazine: Vimy and More, Part 6,* 2004.

Internet: Alumni, University of Toronto, *MacDowell Notes, Charles Dumbrille, Biography of Lieutenant Colonel Thain Wendell MacDowell, V.C., D.S.O. 1890,* 1960.

Journeying in MacDowall Country

Macdowall, Fergus D. H. of Garthland, *The Macdowalls of Galloway*, in *The Tartan*, Clan MacDougall Society of N.A., Fall 1984, vol. 2, no. 9, p. 6, paragraph 9.

MacDowalls of Note

Barnes, Clive, *Dance Magazine*, 2001.

Catton, Bruce, *The Coming Fury*, Pocket Books, Simon & Schuster, New York, 1967.

Current History of the War, New York, New York Times Company, vol.1, December 1914–March 1915.

Fraser, William, *Genealogical Table*, Edinburgh, 1840.

Howard, John, *Our American Music*, Thomas Y. Crowell Co., New York, 1965.

Lever, Tresham, *Lessudden House, Sir Walter Scott and the Scotts of Raeburn*, The Boydell Press, London, 1971.

Macdougal-Hay, Anna-Maria, of Mackerstoun, *Hay-Macdougal of Mackerstoun, Burkes Commoners VIII, A Genealogical and Heraldic History of the Commoners of Great Britain and Ireland*, London, ca. 1830.

Pearson, Hesketh, *Sir Walter Scott*, Harper & Brothers Publishers, New York, 1954.

Prebble, John, *The King's Jaunt: George IV in Scotland, 1822*, William Collins Sons and Co. Ltd., Glasgow, 1988.

Schonberg, Harold C., *The Lives of the Great Composers*, Third Edition, Abacus, London, 2006.

Sullivan, Leo B., Internet, 2007.

Who's Who in America, Marquis Who's Who, New Providence, New Jersey, 2001.

Castles, Towers, and Other Fortified Structures Abbeys of the Lords of Galloway

Agnew, Sir Andrew, *The Hereditary Sheriffs of Galloway, Second Edition,* David Douglas, Edinburgh, 1893.

Chalmers, George, *Caledonia: Or, A Historical and Topographical A Historical And Topographical Account Of North Britain From The Most Ancient To The Present Times, New Edition*, vol. 5, Alexander Gardner, Paisley, Scotland, 1890.

Forsyth, R. O., *The Beauties of Scotland*, vol. 2, Printer John Brown, Edinburgh Scotland, 1805.

Groome, Francis Hind, *Ordnance Gazetteer of Scotland: A Survey of Scottish Topography*, vol. 5, Thomas C. Jack, Grange Publishing Works, Edinburgh, 1884.

Harper, Malcolm Lachlan, *Rambles in Galloway*, Edmonston and Douglas, Edinburgh, 1876.

Hewison, James King, *The Covenanters: A History of the Church in Scotland From The Reformation To The Revolution*, Published By J. Smith and Son, Edinburgh, 1913.

Internet: *Dumfries & Galloway A Gazetteer Of The Region With Places of Interest Including Archaeological, Historical & Protected Sites, Buildings of Note and Nature Reserves*, 2007.

Internet: *Royal Commission on the Ancient and Historical Monuments of Scotland.*

Internet: *The Gazetteer For Scotland.*

Lewis, Samuel, *A Topographical Dictionary of Scotland*, 1846.

Maxwell, Sir Herbert, *A History of Dumfries and Galloway*, William Blackwood and Sons, Edinburgh and London, 1891.

M'Kerlie, P. H., *Galloway in Ancient and Modern Times*, William Blackwood and Sons, Edinburgh and London, 1891.

M'Kerlie, P. H., *History of the Lands and Their Owners in Galloway: With Historical Sketches*, vol. 2, Alexander Gardner, Paisley Scotland, 1906 (Reprint).

Object Name Books of the Ordnance Survey 1874, Book No.149, 33, 36

Salter, Mike, *The Castles of South-West Scotland*, Folly Publications, Malvern, Worcester, 1993.

Society for the Benefit of the Sons and Daughters of the Clergy, *New Statistical Account of Scotland*, vol. 4, Published by W. Blackwood and Sons, Edinburgh and London, 1845.

Society of Antiquaries of Scotland, *Proceedings of the Society of Antiquaries of Scotland, Volume 3, Third Series*, Printed by Neill and Company, Edinburgh, 1893.

Wood, J. Maxwell and Copland, John, *Witchcraft and Superstitious Record in Southwest Scotland*, Kessinger Publishing, Whitefish, Montana, repr. 2003.

Contact Us

Please send comments and your related family history to:

Sheila M. McDowell

35 Hartford Turnpike
Shrewsbury, MA 01545-4592
USA

email: smcdowell@townisp.com

CPSIA information can be obtained
at www.ICGtesting.com
Printed in the USA
BVHW030259260720
584677BV00001B/35